PANDEMIC™

THE ESCAPE-ROOM PUZZLE BOOK

Special thanks to Danielle Robb and Alexander Thieme at Asmodee Entertainment.

Puzzles created by James Hamer-Morton and Charlie Bond.

Published in 2024 by Welbeck
An Imprint of Welbeck Non-Fiction Limited,
part of Welbeck Publishing Group.
Based in London and Sydney.
www.welbeckpublishing.com

A CIP catalogue record for this book is available from the British Library.

ISBN 978 1 80279 181 5

Printed in China

10 9 8 7 6 5 4 3 2 1

PANDEMIC™

THE ESCAPE-ROOM PUZZLE BOOK

CAN YOU SOLVE THE PUZZLES
IN TIME TO SAVE HUMANITY?

JASON WARD

WELBECK

CONTENTS

HOW TO USE THIS BOOK

While their contents vary significantly, there are essentially only two types of puzzle in this book: interconnected Narrative Puzzles that are required for progressing through the story, and self-contained puzzles that can be completed at your own pace.

The interconnected Narrative Puzzles function like an escape room: after reading through a section, you will need to put together different pieces of information to figure out how to find the solution, solving smaller puzzles in order to solve a larger one.

The relevant parts you're looking for can be found only within that chapter and not elsewhere in the book. You must solve a chapter's Narrative Puzzles before moving on to the next chapter.

SOLVE TO PASS

To find the pieces you need, look out for this symbol:

If a puzzle or image doesn't have this symbol, its contents won't be needed anywhere else. There may also be clues in the text.

If you get stuck, a footer on the bottom of the page will guide you to a hint for each part of a puzzle.

FOR A **HINT**, TURN TO PAGE *** • FOR THE **SOLUTION**, TURN TO PAGE ***

Good luck!

PROLOGUE

The first time Sophie Shepherd heard about the pandemic, she didn't even open the article. If she still read a physical newspaper, it would have been halfway to the crossword. A single headline, noted then forgotten:

UNCONFIRMED NEW ILLNESS APPEARS IN JAKARTA

The next week brought "another city, another unread report". An office district had been shut down in Lima. Later on, whenever she tried to remember the timeline, the sequence of events would be fuzzy. She could never quite get the order right; most of it didn't even make the international news. At some point, a group of students were mysteriously ill in Riyadh. A suspected outbreak of food poisoning at a Madrid street festival was baffling local doctors. It was something you became aware of slowly, like background noise getting louder and louder. Your brain tunes out the growing sound until suddenly, it's inescapable. Eventually, you can't hear anything else.

Daily News

Your World. Your News. Now.

UNCONFIRMED NEW ILLNESS APPEARS IN JAKARTA

study of patients in six akarta hoaspitals has vealed up to 13 per cent them had an unexplained fection.

The study tracked 216 tients, showing eight per t had strange symptoms. other five per cent were ly to have had it.

Though most people recovered, they were then struck down with long-term symptoms, the researchers found.

If the results of the study are repeated nationally, many Indonesian patients could be similarly affected by the condition

Humanity owes its existence to a miraculous line of near misses that stretches back, uninterrupted, to our earliest days. For all of the catastrophes and atrocities that colour the past, our history is one of uncanny fortune. Sooner or later, our luck was going to run out.

SUDOKU

CAN YOU FIND THE PERTINENT 5-LETTER WORD?

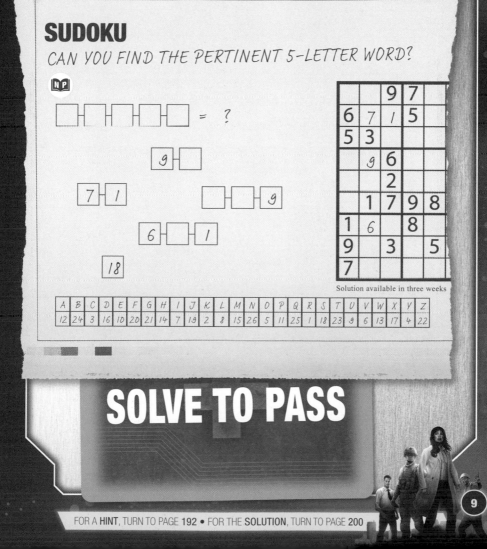

$\square\ \square\ \square\ \square\ \square$ = ?

			9	7			
6	7		1		5			
5	3							
				9	6			
				2				
			1	7		9	8	
1		6			8			
9			3				5	
7								

Solution available in three weeks

A	B	C	D	E	F	G	H	I	J	K	L	M	N	O	P	Q	R	S	T	U	V	W	X	Y	Z
12	24	3	16	10	20	21	14	7	19	2	8	15	26	5	11	25	1	18	23	9	6	13	17	4	22

SOLVE TO PASS

CHAPTER 1

GLOBAL HEALTH AGENCY

ATLANTA

CHAPTER 1: GLOBAL HEALTH AGENCY, ATLANTA

Becoming a Troubleshooter had been a kind of waking dream. Sophie Shepherd felt like it had been created especially for her out of her passions and best qualities – as if she'd done a career aptitude test at school and they'd proceeded to fashion an entire profession out of her results. The only problem with being one, she thought, was everything except the actual troubleshooting.

The issue was the title. "Troubleshooter" made promises that no amount of keen prognostication could match. As proud as she was of her work, she worried that it looked silly on a lanyard, particularly when you were surrounded by virologists and epidemiologists and those who somehow understood the difference between the two. At her old workplace – it still felt strange saying that – colleagues would frequently think she was there to fix the computers, or would come to her about territorial disputes in the staff fridge.

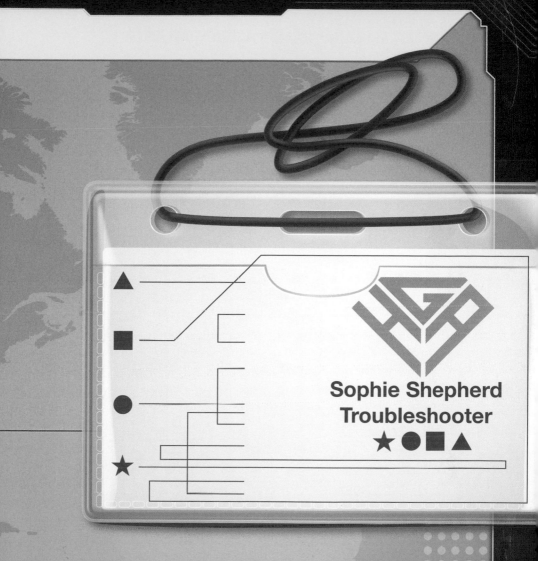

Sophie Shepherd
Troubleshooter
★ ● ■ ▲

SHEPHERD ANALYZED HER GLOBAL HEALTH AGENCY ID CARD SHE RECEIVED IN THE POST.

WAS THERE A HIDDEN MESSAGE?

13

FOR A **HINT**, TURN TO PAGE **192** • FOR THE **SOLUTION**, TURN TO PAGE **200**

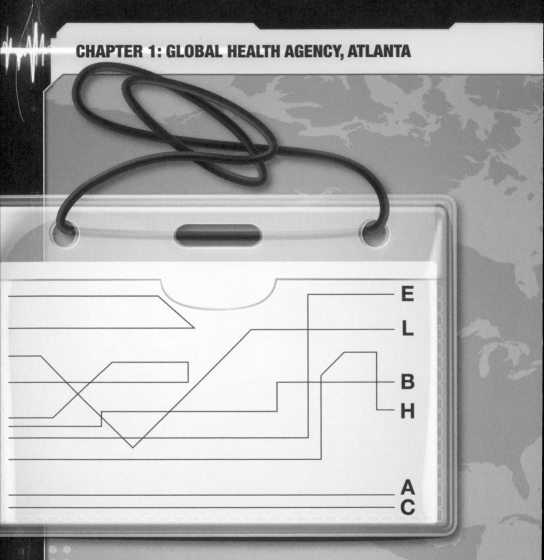

That she was adept at solving both of these complaints was beside the point. She had a rare talent for being able to see an intransigent situation in a new way, to somehow transform a problem into its own solution. She thought of it as being able to see a little further around the bend, spotting approaching obstacles before they came into view.

As the shuttle bus rounded its turn, Shepherd glimpsed the Global Health Agency's (GHA) Atlanta headquarters for the first time. Until now, she had only worked at local agency offices. The GHA was a genuine wonder of the modern age, but from the outside it looked like a new university campus, or a mall complex defying the gravity of online shopping. There was nothing to suggest that it was housing one of the nation's most significant agencies, with an operating budget that ran into the billions.

The industry gossip – the gossip of multiple industries, in fact – was that GHA had been quietly vacuuming up talent on an unprecedented scale. Shepherd hadn't even been interviewed for her job. It felt more like conscription than recruitment: phone call on Friday, new life on Monday. She assumed she'd be helping tackle the disease that had popped up in a few cities, but the secrecy and scale of it all was disconcerting. She didn't need to be a Troubleshooter to understand that all this would only be happening if there was something very, very wrong.

It would be easy to get lost in such a huge organisation, but Shepherd hoped that the other industry gossip was also true: that the GHA was the kind of place where your abilities could be recognised and actually appreciated. At the very least, hopefully no-one would ask her how to clear a printer jam. On the way to the main complex, the bus passed a string of five buildings – staff accommodation, perhaps, as they all currently seemed empty, aside from lights illuminating a single floor in each building. A tower stood at the front, eleven storeys tall, with a walkway between the sixth and seventh floors, and a lit-up third floor. The next building was smaller: eight levels, with a gap after the third, and only the ground floor illuminated. The shortest building came next, with the top of its five storeys lit up. Next came an eight-storey building, its seventh floor aglow, and finally, 12 full storeys of homesick scientists, its fifth level illuminated. Clearly, this group of buildings was where the action was, but Shepherd was relieved that Atlanta also boasted her accommodating sister and her spare room.

• • • •

To my successor

No one was coming. There'd been no one to meet her at reception either, and clearly no one would be inducting her anytime soon. Upon Shepherd's arrival, it became obvious that the GHA primarily comprised several hundred experts in varying degrees of panic. It wasn't disarray, exactly – more a sort of focused pandemonium, a storm before the storm.

Thankfully, she had been given a designated desk location in advance. Shepherd rifled through her desk drawers, looking for some kind of handover document. She didn't even have a login for her computer. The cubicle was bare except for a map of the world, webbed with lines connecting dozens of major cities.

404-706-0539

2928 LIMER STREET,
ATLANTA, GEORGIA

GHA.2MAN

To my successor,

Welcome to the GHA.

The IT department keep telling me not to leave four-digit codes lying around, but I spotted something in today's newspaper that might be of some interest.

20,5,9,1,18,7,17,22,10,1,5,23,13,5

Sorry I couldn't be there for a proper handover. No doubt our paths will cross in the future.

Good luck.

To my successor

At the bottom of a drawer she found an unsealed envelope. The note was perplexing. Shepherd thought maybe it would give her the password for the computer, but she couldn't believe that GHA's HR protocols would be so inefficient and unprofessional. They were the most essential branch of the Global Health Agency, the pre-eminent international agency for the prevention and control of disease – if their staff had to solve a puzzle just to check their emails, nobody would ever get anything done.

Shepherd figured out how to use the numbers. She entered the four digits into the computer. Nothing. Oh well. It was worth a try. Maybe a former employee had just been really into puzzles. She returned the letter back to the envelope and tossed the envelope back into the drawer and headed for the data hub.

A bank of monitors stretched across the back wall. It displayed a live version of the map in her office: disease hotspots, the spread of outbreaks, teams of medics and researchers moving from city to city. Beyond the curious Dutch spelling "Khartoem", she didn't immediately clock the difference between the two versions, but when she did, her legs went weak. She could hear the blood roaring in her ears.

There were four different colours on the map.

Everything clicked into place. The GHA hadn't been hiring half of the world's medical experts to deal with one new disease, but to deal with *four*: Black, Yellow, Red, Blue. The unimaginable had happened...and then it had happened three more times, simultaneously. She needed to sit down. She needed to weep. She needed to help.

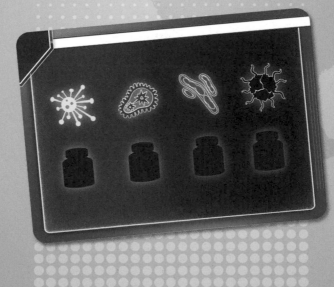

The map dwarfed her. She could barely take in the whole thing at once, and this was just an illustration. It was all too complicated, too overwhelming. She took a deep breath. If the GHA didn't have time to interview her, she didn't have time to doubt herself. This was her moment to live up to the job title on her lanyard.

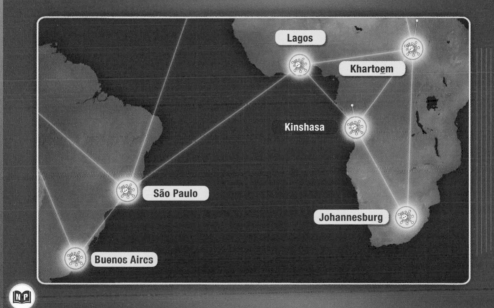

FOR A **HINT**, TURN TO PAGE **192** • FOR THE **SOLUTION**, TURN TO PAGE **202**

For a start, the medics were being sent to the wrong places. Unless action was taken imminently, an outbreak was coming. Trouble had poked its head around the bend. She needed to tell someone which city needed to be protected, right now.

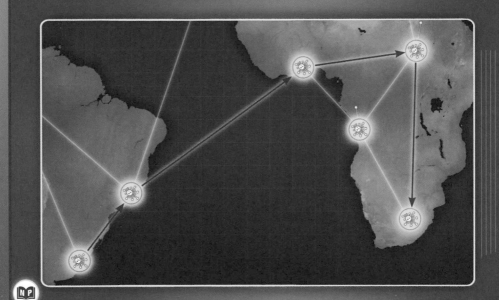

FOR A **HINT**, TURN TO PAGE 192 • FOR THE **SOLUTION**, TURN TO PAGE 202

SOLVE TO PASS

CHAPTER 2

DISPATCHER RESPONSE UNIT

ATLANTA

This is what it must feel like to be a house in a wildfire, thought Yasuo Shōnagon. He watched the woman bound from desk to desk, creeping up the mountain to torch his day. He didn't recognize her, but the GHA had taken on so many new staff lately it would be more unusual if he did. The sudden influx spoke to the scale of their situation.

THERE IS A BROKEN DEVICE WHICH ISN'T DISPLAYING THE USER NAME CORRECTLY.

WHO DOES IT BELONG TO?

The scale of their ambition did too, he supposed. Every new colleague he met was smart, talented and thoughtful, but every new colleague also wanted him to pull off some impossible task. One of his original colleagues pointed in his direction – never a good sign. She caught his eye and smiled, a gesture somehow both friendly and anxious.

"Essen! Essen!" she said. "Hi, sorry, it's my first day. I'm Sophie Shepherd...and your map is wrong."

"Yasuo Shōnagon. Welcome to the Dispatcher Response Unit (DRU). How do you mean?"

"You're a Dispatcher, yes? We have to dispatch! Medics, Researchers, Containment Specialists, I'll even take Generalists if you've got them. An outbreak in Essen could spread to Paris, Milan, St Petersburg, London. We'd lose Europe in a week to...does it have a name?"

It did have a name, but like the three other diseases that had emerged alongside it, that name couldn't actually be pronounced – D8C1T1 – a jumbled eruption of letters and numbers that would be the start of a decent password but was otherwise unusable. Although Shōnagon assumed that better names would similarly rise from the ether, the colours from the map had stuck, at least around the DRU.

"Blue is fine."

"I'm a Troubleshooter, by the way. Did I say that? My role is to–"

"You identify problems that the rest of us *can't even see*, and then you solve them. I'd say it's the most important job here if I didn't have a healthy respect for the entire team, both here and abroad."

His new colleague smiled to herself curiously, then turned towards the map. Back to work.

Shōnagon had a limited number of resources that would change depending on the disease classification itself; how severe the outbreak was, and had a number of options of how to use them. They needed to get a Medic, a Researcher, a Generalist and a Containment Specialist to Essen. The three options were to Drive, Charter a flight or Transfer between research stations. Something would tell him how many of each he could use.

A **D**rive resource would allow any person to move one space on the map, whether driving across land or moving over water.

A **C**hartered flight would take any person from their current position directly to another city. Unfortunately, the only flights available to charter at this time need to head to St Petersburg as their destination.

A **T**ransfer would take any person who was at a research station (marked by a white "building" on the map) to any other research station in the world.

FOR A **HINT**, TURN TO PAGE **192** • FOR THE **SOLUTION**, TURN TO PAGE **203**

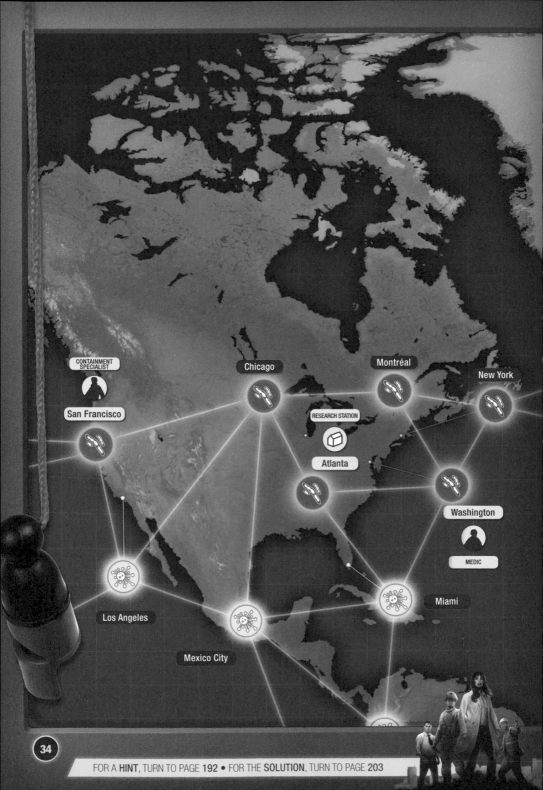

CONTAINMENT
SPECIALIST

San Francisco

Chicago

Montréal

New York

RESEARCH STATION

Atlanta

Washington

MEDIC

Los Angeles

Miami

Mexico City

34

FOR A **HINT**, TURN TO PAGE **192** • FOR THE **SOLUTION**, TURN TO PAGE **203**

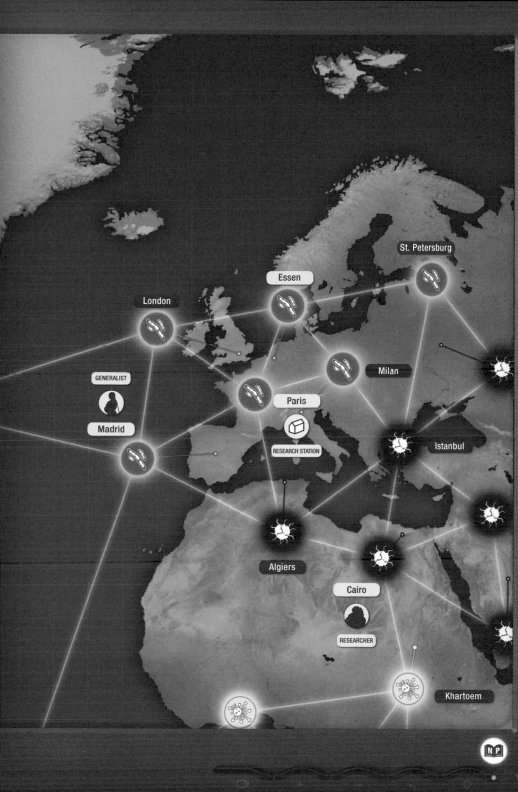

Shōnagon took a special note on which person used what resources, but managed to get everyone to Essen in time, and drew his results with his index finger on the chart on the wall to make sure he was right.

IF CONTAINMENT SPECIALIST OR GENERALIST USES A CHARTERED FLIGHT, MOVE LEFT.

IF RESEARCHER OR MEDIC USES A CHARTERED FLIGHT, MOVE RIGHT.

IF CONTAINMENT SPECIALIST OR GENERALIST USES A TRANSFER, MOVE LEFT.

IF RESEARCHER OR MEDIC USES A TRANSFER FLIGHT, MOVE RIGHT.

MOVE LEFT THE NUMBER OF DRIVE RESOURCES USED BY THE CONTAINMENT SPECIALIST.

MOVE RIGHT THE NUMBER OF DRIVE RESOURCES USED BY THE MEDIC.

MOVE LEFT THE NUMBER OF DRIVE RESOURCES USED BY THE RESEARCHER.

MOVE RIGHT THE NUMBER OF DRIVE RESOURCES USED BY THE GENERALIST.

With a flurry of taps, he entered the information to send the staff on their way. There, done.

Shepherd slumped down on the chair next to him and seemed to exhale all of the air from her body. This was a good morning.

Shōnagon sincerely thought that logistics were humanity's greatest accomplishment. It was the invisible thread holding together an unfathomably large and complicated world, keeping food on the shelves and medicine in the hospitals. His passion made him excited about topics that would have bored others – shipping routes, refineries, supply chains. Even the other dispatchers couldn't hope to match his fervour. They called him "the Conductor" because he kept the trains running; as a joke they once got him a wooden train whistle for his birthday, and he took it with him everywhere.

TO REMEMBER THE COMPLICATED WAY TO HIS OFFICE, SHŌNAGON USES A SPECIAL WORD – BUT SOMETIMES HE GETS THE LETTERS IN A SCRAMBLE.

ROUTE TO OFFICE

FOR A **HINT**, TURN TO PAGE **192** • FOR THE **SOLUTION**, TURN TO PAGE **204**

There was no greater sight than the DRU live map in motion, as personnel and equipment traversed the globe to where they were needed most, like pieces in a board game. He liked the element of trust that working for such a substantial organization demanded. It was like logistics in miniature: the health care and scientific staff that he transported relied on him to move them to the right place, and he relied on them to do the correct work when they got there. Everyone depended on everyone else, and so everyone mattered.

SHŌNAGON'S BACKPACK IS CURRENTLY LOCKED WITH A
FOUR-DIGIT CODE. BUT THERE IS ALWAYS A HINT, IN CASE
IT'S FORGOTTEN.

$$Q\,E\,Y$$
$$+\,Q\,Q\,Y$$
$$+\,E\,Q\,Y$$
$$\overline{=\,E\,Q\,Q\,Y}$$

SOLVE TO PASS

FOR A HINT, TURN TO PAGE 192 • FOR THE SOLUTION, TURN TO PAGE 204

CONSTRUCTION SITE

HO CHI MINH CITY

As the train blocked the street, Joe Saunders wondered what he used to think about before the pandemic. It wasn't as if he previously had endless time to ruminate or lived a life free of burdens. He still worried about all the things he used to worry about, but he couldn't remember what else used to occupy that space now devoted to infection rates and population immunity. It certainly didn't feel like anything had been pushed out. Maybe worry was like an overflow car park – there's always a little extra space for emergencies.

"TÌNH HUỐNG XẤU NHẤT"

He wasn't alone. The near miss in Essen had reverberated far beyond the Ruhr. Even though Essen had evaded disaster, it was clear that others wouldn't be as lucky. Every day brought another outbreak and more fires to be extinguished, the four diseases expanding their territories city by city.

Nowhere had "fallen" yet, but it seemed unavoidable that bad timing and neighbouring outbreaks would eventually nudge a city over the edge. This would be catastrophic enough, but a growing concern was that it would set off a chain reaction both uncontrollable and unparalleled. While there was a rare sense of global unanimity, the phrase "worst-case scenario" had started appearing in normal conversations with alarming regularity.

CHAPTER 3: CONSTRUCTION SITE, HO CHI MINH CITY

THE HOTEL ROOM ON SAUNDERS' FLOOR WERE UNUSUALLY NUMBERED, BUT THEY SEEMED TO FOLLOW A SEQUENCE.

WHAT ROOM WAS HE IN?

3

?

7

10

9

11

8

23

6

4

14

27

FOR A **HINT**, TURN TO PAGE 192 • FOR THE **SOLUTION**, TURN TO PAGE 205

A newfound vigilance wasn't the only dividend of the pandemic: the GHA's decisive actions had gifted them the political weight to build a network of research stations in key cities. For better or worse, this was now their crisis to resolve. As an Operations Expert, Saunders wasn't just on the frontline of this battle, he was also the one building it. The breadth of their problems demanded a concerted approach, which meant the research stations needed to be intricately coordinated.

Saunders and his team were essentially building the same institution over and over again, dispatched by "the Conductor of Atlanta" to whichever city might be best placed to yield results. A scientist heading to work in Lima probably had no idea that another scientist in Khartoum was heading to an identical building, using the same parking spot, sitting at the same desk, throwing crumpled paper into the same bin.

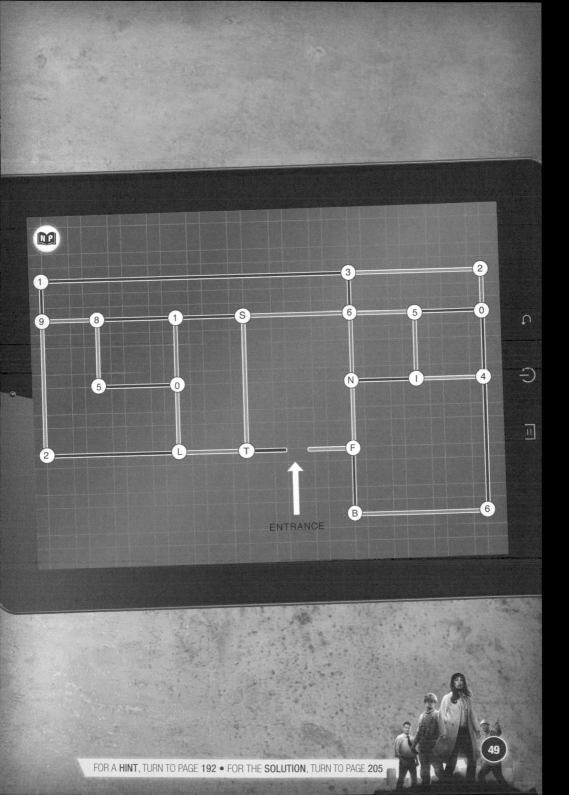

ENTRANCE

49

The idea amused Saunders, but maybe it was just that he was entering the third month of his slow world tour. Except for the snacks in the vending machines, the only functional difference was a framed line drawing, which always hung in the same spot in the break room.

Drawn by Saunders at night after he'd left the site, it depicted a few of the local workers who'd helped out during the construction. He assumed it would be taken down by the end of the first day, but it was as close to a signature as he could get. It felt important to have some recognition that each city was living through its own pandemic. The people themselves weren't indistinguishable, even if the buildings were.

FOR A **HINT**, TURN TO PAGE **192** • FOR THE **SOLUTION**, TURN TO PAGE **205**

He was quietly proud of his latest work. When he looked at it, he could remember exactly where he'd been on the day it depicted: the sun on the back of his neck, the dull throb of the jet-lag. He remembered that he'd seemingly spent that whole morning surveying his train options, trying to determine the correct one to take. The traffic had been no better back then, either.

THÔNG TIN TÀU HỎA – TRAIN INFORMATION

ĐƠN HÀNG – Order	SỐ TÀU – Train Number	NƠI ĐẾN – DESTINATION
1	FB643	SÀI GÒN
2	FN630	DĨ AN
3	TL169	THỦ ĐỨC
4	FN261	BÌNH TRIỆU
5	TS105	SÓNG THẦN
6	TL293	GÒ VẤP
7	TS510	SÀI GÒN
8	FB502	DĨ AN

The train left, allowing him to finally exit his accommodation. He'd seen a lot of the world recently – mostly the parts containing construction sites, admittedly – but every new place, with its novel banalities, brought something he found thrilling. Was it common in Ho Chi Minh City for apartment buildings to open straight on to train tracks, or was that just a quirk of his street? The other residents seemed unperturbed, but the building planner in his head couldn't help but try to figure out the complex history that had led scooters to the roads and trains to the streets.

FOR A **HINT**, TURN TO PAGE 192 • FOR THE **SOLUTION**, TURN TO PAGE 206

Where did the French colonial buildings fit in, or the modernist apartment blocks, or those that came after reunification? What of the three-digit numbers painted on to the trees? Allegedly, they helped manage the rate of tree planting, but surely that would also be a decent alibi for all sorts of other purposes for the numbers. They seem so separate, nature and industry, but the trees are connected to the buildings whether they want to be or not. A city was an ongoing story to be read, and he supposed that this research station was his chapter.

When his team arrived in Ho Chi Minh City, Saunders had just crested the ridge of overconfidence. The uniformity of the stations meant the team could be fairly precise about timings – he didn't just know the day they'd finish, he believed it would be late afternoon. So it was inevitable that things would start going wrong. Sometimes materials wouldn't arrive, or crews would be diverted to the wrong locations. One day a gang of joiners even turned up in the nearby city of Vũng Tàu instead for reasons that nobody could work out.

FOR A **HINT**, TURN TO PAGE **193** • FOR THE **SOLUTION**, TURN TO PAGE **206**

If the delays had been worse, perhaps none of this would have gotten Saunders's attention. Good weather always turns eventually, and they'd had sunshine for months. Instead, there was something conspicuously inconspicuous about it all, as if the chaos was pitched just below the threshold of perception. Once it had gotten into his head, he couldn't quite shake the notion that there was something almost *deliberate* about the complications. But why would anyone be interested in hindering the construction of a research station, and if they were going to, why would they do it in such an underhanded fashion?

SAUNDERS HAS ASKED FOR A SNACK FROM THE VENDING MACHINE, AND HANDS YOU THIS STRANGE SET OF NUMBERS. WHAT SNACK DOES HE WANT?

ĐỒ ĂN NHẸ
SNACKS

D1
A3
C1
B3
A2

Eats — A1
Munch — A2
Break — A3

Yums — B1
Scran — B2
Tasty — B3

Plang — C1
SLOPS — C2
NOMS — C3

Cronch — D1
Snakk — D2
Helth — D3

59

FOR A **HINT**, TURN TO PAGE **193** • FOR THE **SOLUTION**, TURN TO PAGE **206**

CHAPTER 3: CONSTRUCTION SITE, HO CHI MINH CITY

The project had lost a few days, at most. It was almost like a...
Saunders couldn't find the word, which is probably why he'd drafted
and discarded several emails on the subject to various colleagues
at the GHA. He was paranoid, surely. He'd just been on the road too
long – this probably happened to rock bands all the time.

He entered the half-finished station and his paranoia returned, the
feeling rising up through his feet. There weren't just a few workers
missing this time – they were all gone. Saunders made circuits of
the building, like a man checking his pocket for lost keys over and
over again. He ticked off the possibilities. The trains were clearly still
running. It wasn't monsoon season, so there was no chance of tropical
cyclones. Maybe there was a national holiday no one had told him
about? He returned to the entrance. The paranoia had made it to his
chest; the gate was now locked by a keypad. He was stuck, or at least
he told himself he was stuck, because that was less alarming than the
word *trapped*.

An accident, then, and what an extraordinary accident to happen two days before the other entrances were usable, and on the very day that the phone lines were supposed to be installed. A reasonable person in this situation might conclude that someone was toying with them. Presumably, that reasonable person would also try to put such thoughts out of their mind until they'd extricated themselves.

Saunders looked at the keypad: it required a four-digit code. He couldn't jump the gate, but he was willing to use his initiative to solve the problem. He had a feeling that he just might be able to deduce the code, if he could just see the forest for the trees.

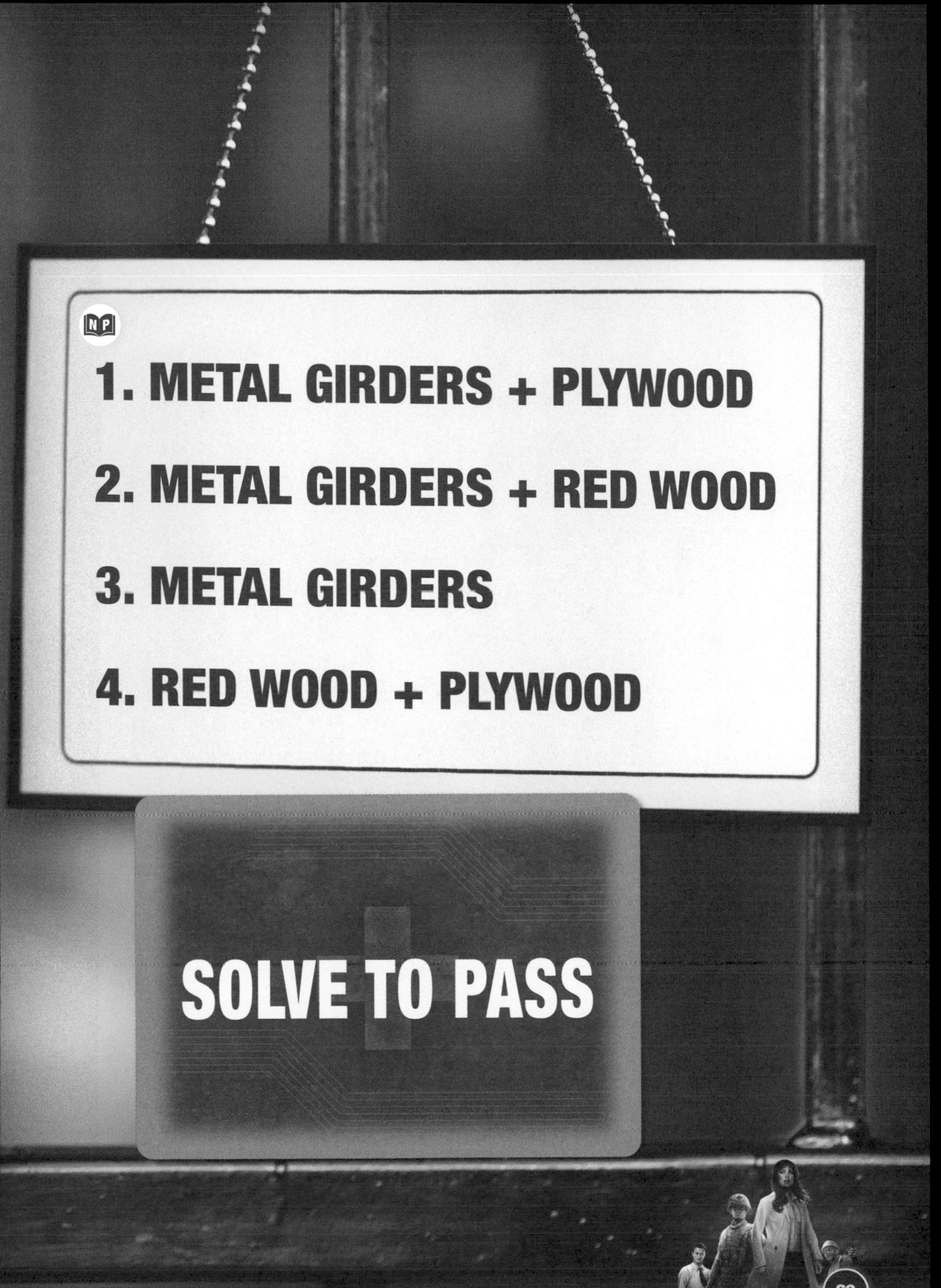

1. **METAL GIRDERS + PLYWOOD**

2. **METAL GIRDERS + RED WOOD**

3. **METAL GIRDERS**

4. **RED WOOD + PLYWOOD**

SOLVE TO PASS

FOR A **HINT**, TURN TO PAGE **193** • FOR THE **SOLUTION**, TURN TO PAGE **206**

RESEARCH STATION

MILAN

They called it "the Quiet Night". After weeks of rising numbers on every continent, the pandemic had stalled. While infection rates remained daunting, the four diseases were no longer spreading to other cities.

There was no apparent reason for it – diseases don't call ceasefires – but after all the panic and strife, it was a small blessing. The public, in their more optimistic moments, expressed hope that this was the high-water mark, the beginning of the end. Deep down, of course, everyone knew that this was likely just the end of the beginning. Something to be valued, certainly, but merely an untroubled watch before everything kicked off again in the morning.

CAN YOU SORT THROUGH THE DATA TO FIGURE OUT THE INFECTIONS (IN 1,000S OF PEOPLE) FOR EACH SEPARATE DISEASE? *N.B. WHOLE NUMBERS ONLY.*

🦠	🦠	🦠	11
🦠	🦠	🦠	12
🦠	🦠		10
14	5	14	

🦠 = ?
🦠 = ?
🦠 = ?
🦠 = ?

" ELIMINATE SADNESS "

DON'T FEEL BLUE

FOR A **HINT**, TURN TO PAGE **193** • FOR THE **SOLUTION**, TURN TO PAGE **207**

CHAPTER 4: RESEARCH STATION, MILAN

For Ewa Tokarczuk, the Quiet Night was an invitation to be ambitious. As the lead scientist at the Milan Research Station, her work had mostly concentrated on potential treatments. Her staff had been trying to keep their heads above water, but now they had a chance to actually focus on a cure for the "Blue" disease recently tearing through Europe and North America.

Who knew how long a night could last, she wondered? During those long winters growing up in Lodz, morning never seemed to come, but in Milan she would routinely wake to a city that had already had a brioche and an espresso. She concluded that it was easy to take metaphors a little too far.

CDeOC

WLnBr

SbVrH

PsRsE

DPCJp

FOR A **HINT**, TURN TO PAGE **193** • FOR THE **SOLUTION**, TURN TO PAGE **207**

Age of Sample
38

Age of Sample
22

Age of Sample
48

FOR A **HINT**, TURN TO PAGE **193** • FOR THE **SOLUTION**, TURN TO PAGE **207**

CHAPTER 4: RESEARCH STATION, MILAN

Essen's narrow escape had been a warning to the world, but Tokarczuk was convinced that it was also an opportunity. Data was only just starting to arrive from the city's hospitals and quarantined districts. A picture was emerging of how the disease had first spread, and how it had been temporarily driven off. If she could figure out why the medics had been more successful in Essen than in comparable places, maybe she could apply those lessons directly to the cure. Somewhere in this data was a breakthrough, just waiting to be found.

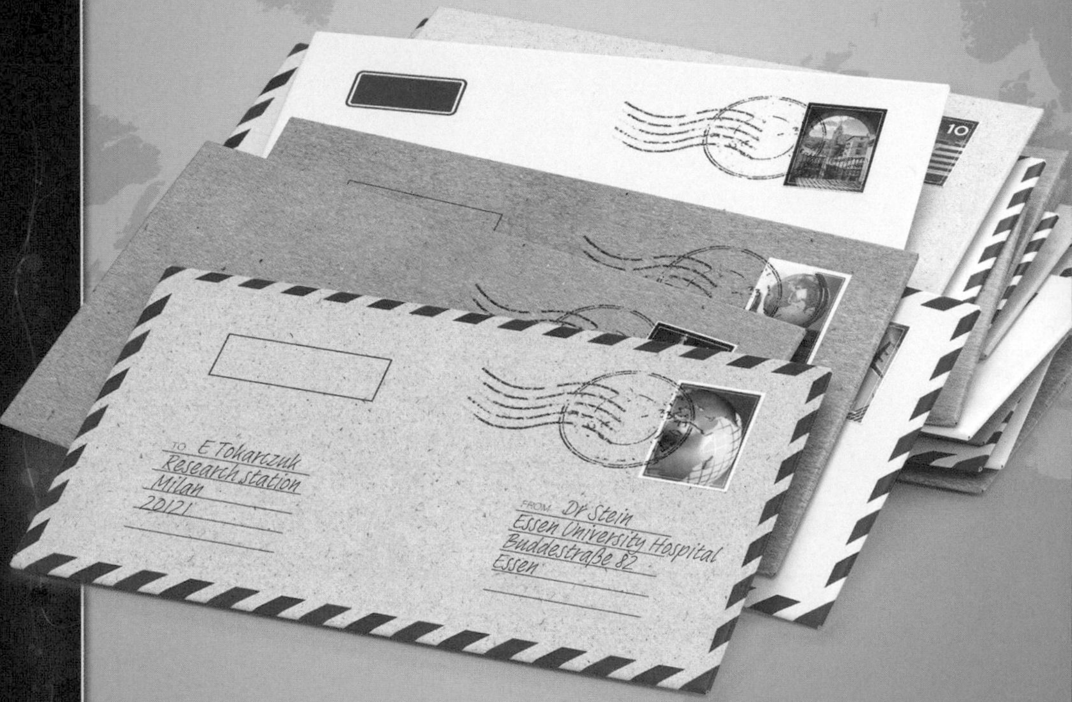

TO E Tokarczuk
Research station
Milan
20121
FROM Dr Stein
Essen University Hospital
Buddestraße 82
Essen

ESSEN
UNIVERSITY HOSPITAL

Dear Ewa,

I've asked my assistant to enclose the list of cases from our hospital. I'm tending a small hope that something in the results will show an effective treatment from the right cocktail of drugs.

The case in question (I do not have the information in front of me – they were definitely named Gerry or Lou) was astounding. The patient became non-infectious so swiftly that the attending doctor assumed it was an error. Imagine if it wasn't.

We can't get to the bottom of it, but hopefully you'll have more luck.

Dr Stein

Essen University Hospital

(+49) 201 8791583

essen@iubridge.com

Essen University Hospital
Buddestraße 82, Essen

73

Tokarczuk leaned back in her chair, turning it bipedal until the voice of her mother – never that far away, lurking in the next room, perhaps – told her to stop. She'd never been any good at taking breaks.

TOKARCZUK DECIDES TO ORDER TAKEOUT, BUT HER NEW CREDIT CARD HAS BEEN DAMAGED.

WHAT ARE THE LAST FOUR DIGITS?

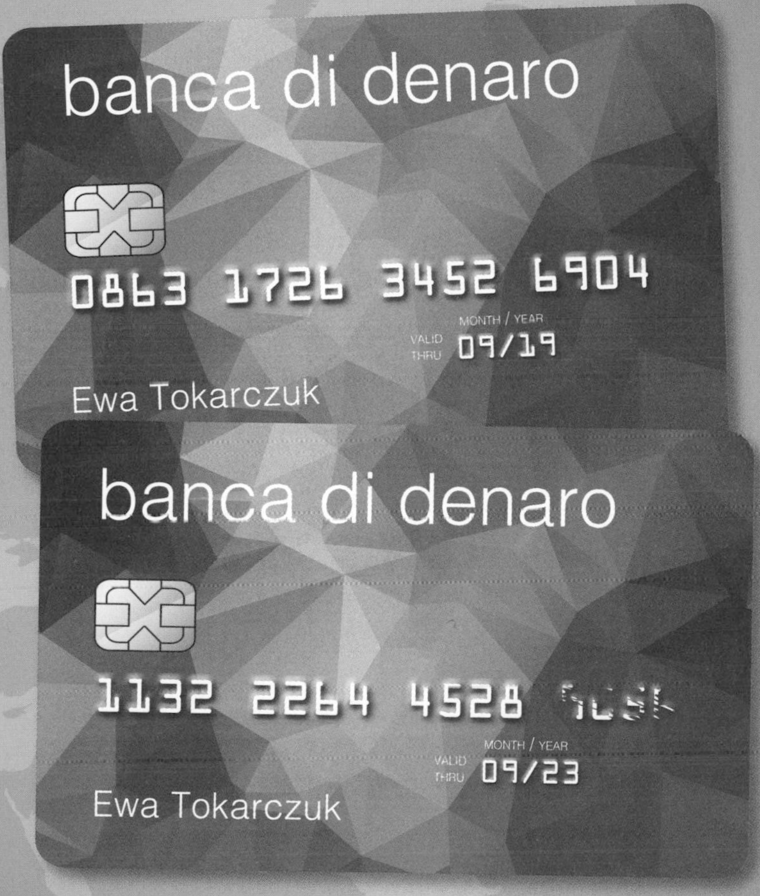
banca di denaro
0863 1726 3452 6904
MONTH / YEAR
VALID THRU 09/19
Ewa Tokarczuk
banca di denaro
1132 2264 4528
MONTH / YEAR
VALID THRU 09/23
Ewa Tokarczuk

FOR A **HINT**, TURN TO PAGE **193** • FOR THE **SOLUTION**, TURN TO PAGE **207**

Her lunches had been habitually conducted at her desk, crumbs fluttering down into her keyboard, until her team threatened strike action, demanding she eat in the break room.

This was unrealistic and melodramatic, she thought, but she took their point. At least it'd give her leverage about working weekends, the other apparent crime they took issue with. Now, instead of one of the most crucial problems facing humanity, she could direct her attention to...a drawing of some men in hard hats, with their faces doodled on so they were now smiling ambiguously.

THE PASSWORD TO TOKARCZUK'S PC IS SO EASY TO GUESS!

HER KEYBOARD IS WORN DOWN FROM TYPING SO MUCH.

FOR A **HINT**, TURN TO PAGE **193** • FOR THE **SOLUTION**, TURN TO PAGE **208**

She did have to admit (not to her staff, obviously) that the breaks were productive. Some problems you solve with hard work, but others you have to sneak up on, or let the answers reveal themselves to you. This could be as true of medical research as it was of creative endeavours. Take, for instance, her current predicament. The list of cases from Essen had come through, but without specifying the successful cocktail of drugs that provoked antibodies. If she could eliminate the cases that weren't correct, she would be left with one final cocktail that was the cure. The solution had proven as elusive to her as it had to everyone else, but maybe she just needed to listen to the hum of the vending machine while her mind discreetly put everything together. It was within her grasp – she knew it.

Test Subject Results (Batch 30)

Case no.	Name	Age	D.O.B.	Location	Cocktail given	Antibodies?
174264	G. Müller	28	24th July	Essen	WPVsp-18	...
296477	L. Richter	34	12th February	Essen	DLerE-16	...
197520	W. Klein	38	28th May	Essen	CbnJH-11	...
294164	G. Hartman	28	14th June	Essen	PsCFe-19	...
274314	L. Bauer	28	1st November	Essen	SDKOr-15	...
247241	P. Werner	34	15th January	Essen	LsRBC-14	...
341311	L. Hoffman	38	25th September	Essen	SDKOr-05	...
187800	G. Vogel	22	19th January	Essen	WPVsp-09	...
246161	M. Freidrich	38	19th April	Essen	LsRBC-18	...
105772	L. Weiß	48	5th June	Essen	SDKOr-06	...
199825	G. Ludwig	38	29th March	Essen	DLerE-15	...
124164	H. Otto	28	2nd March	Essen	DLerE-13	...

SOLVE TO PASS

FOR A **HINT**, TURN TO PAGE 193 • FOR THE **SOLUTION**, TURN TO PAGE 208

CHAPTER 5

TREATMENT CAMP
ISTANBUL

PART ONE

Doug Vowell still found it amazing that names for viruses took hold in previous pandemics before the invention of the printing press. When a disease could wipe out a third of Europe without breaking a sweat, how did everyone agree what to call it? One Christmas, he'd been given a book containing a list of gloriously antiquated maladies – King's Evil, Ristling, Tiffick, Rising of the Lights – but even among that dishevelled collection of folk ailments, there seemed to be some consensus.

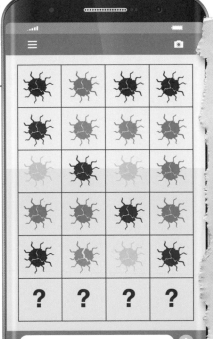

Row 1: One colour is correct, but not in the right place

Row 2: One colour is correct, and in the right place. One colour is correct, but in the wrong place.

Row 3: One colour is correct, and in the right place. One colour is correct, but in the wrong place.

Row 4: One colour is correct, but not in the right place.

Row 5: One colour is correct, and in the right place. Three colours are correct, but in the wrong place.

IN WHICH ORDER WERE THE VIRUSES DISCOVERED?

The convoluted scientific names for the four diseases had left a void that no one could quite fill. Existing as four linked but separate entities, perhaps there were too many options. Spring, Summer, Autumn, Winter? Clubs, Diamonds, Hearts, Spades? Dorothy, Scarecrow, Tin Woodman, Cowardly Lion? John, Paul, George, Ringo? No one could agree. A shorthand was necessary, but naming deadly diseases after the Golden Girls, Ninja Turtles or the Pac-Man ghosts seemed in poor taste – everywhere except on social media.

Perhaps it should be called Momibaal?

Or at least Mo-Mi-Ba-Al...

In the end, most people just ended up referring to them by the colours of the GHA dispatcher map, which had been a prominent early image of the pandemic. You knew where you stood: if you were in South America, you worried about Yellow, if you were in Europe you worried about Blue, and if you were in Istanbul you worried about basically everything.

Essen

London

Paris

Madrid

Algiers

St. Petersburg

Milan

Moscow

Istanbul

Cairo

Baghdad

FOR A **HINT**, TURN TO PAGE **194** • FOR THE **SOLUTION**, TURN TO PAGE **209**

Vowell had arrived in the city three days earlier. Medics were needed in every country, but Istanbul's health services were reeling from outbreak after outbreak. It was unsurprising that they faced multiple fronts. Istanbul was one of history's great cities because it was on the edge of everything, a vibrant confluence straddling both Asia and Europe.

Over the centuries, this had made it the heart of several empires, but had left it vulnerable geographically. Black was emphatically the disease in residence, but Blue was knocking on the door, and who knew? Maybe Yellow would eventually pay a visit. As much they tried to resist, it was hard to avoid war analogies: arriving into the Bosphorus strait by skiff, via hospital ship, Vowell felt like a conscript in a losing war.

THE INFECTION REPORT WAS CONCLUSIVE.

FIND AN EIGHT-LETTER WORD TO PASS.

INFECTION REPORT

ANALYSIS

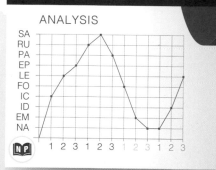

SA
RU
PA
EP
LE
FO
IC
ID
EM
NA

1 2 3 1 2 3 1 2 3 1 2 3

SOLVE TO PASS

⚠ EPIDEMIC

1. INCREASE
Our infection rate has increased. Daily we are seeing more cities' numbers go through the **roof**.

2. INFECT
One city in particular has fallen **foul** to a complete infection. We must do everything in our power to mitigate the threat of this spreading to others with a full outbreak.

3. INTENSIFY
Perhaps through a mutation or variant, it seems that further infections could hit even cities that have already seen a **peak** beforehand.

FOR A **HINT**, TURN TO PAGE 194 • FOR THE **SOLUTION**, TURN TO PAGE 210

PART TWO

The jubilation caused by Blue's cure was short-lived, or at least tempered by shabby reality, as the world remembered that curing a disease is one thing, but eradicating it is quite another – after all, you could still go to parts of the American West and catch the bubonic plague from a prairie dog. Blue continued to rage through two continents, spreading as fast as it could be exterminated. Their efforts weren't in vain, but the journey was going to be longer than anyone had hoped.

With every hospital full to capacity, makeshift treatment camps had been set up in vacant stadiums and conference centres across the city. At Vowell's camp, there were still posters for the cancelled gigs that would no longer take place.

FOR A **HINT**, TURN TO PAGE **194** • FOR THE **SOLUTION**, TURN TO PAGE **210**

In ideal circumstances, Angie Parker would have been the first person in Istanbul to hear about the new epidemic, but the world had long been a stranger to ideal circumstances. All at once, a million phones hummed with dread. Parker's was just one of them. The news was frightening: Karachi had finally "fallen" and infections were surging across the region, with rates now only slightly slower than the panic rippling out ahead.

As she'd walked among them, the people of Istanbul had had no idea of the responsibility she held over their lives. The Global Health Agency had endowed Parker with as much authority as the city's mayor or governor. A Quarantine Specialist was able to lock down streets, districts or even the whole city if she needed to. She could close the bridges and ports with a phone call. It wasn't a power she enjoyed or took lightly. Her actions would have immediate, tangible effects on the lives of millions, including – she noted as the phone in her pocket continued to buzz – herself and all of her colleagues scattered in treatment camps across the city.

Angie Parker

.ooo01 4G   09.59 🔋

15 Mar

C. Besnard
Great work today, Ange. Maybe we really do have a shot. Let's just contain what we can for now, and hopefully buy some time for a cure

17 Mar

B. Samwell
Hey, I'm a little concerned by the latest from the GHA… have we really not hit our peak yet?

23 Mar

K. Sahin
I'm standing on my roof and it's all so peaceful, like a regular spring day. I'm stunned by how well the city has responded to your plans. Thank you. Let's hope this works.

25 Mar

B. Samwell
Sorry to hear about Istanbul. Let me know if you'd like some of our data, I can fly over any time.

26 Mar

S. Shepherd
I know! One would be bad enough, but four? It's foul, is what it is.

28 Mar

S. Shepherd
OUTBREAK IN KARACHI!
Call Shön ASAP.

28 Mar

I. Parker
Dad just told me about Karachi –
are you okay? x

Write a message   ➕

93

FOR A **HINT**, TURN TO PAGE **194** • FOR THE **SOLUTION**, TURN TO PAGE **210**

CHAPTER 5: TREATMENT CAMP, ISTANBUL

A Troubleshooter called Shepherd, apparently convinced that Istanbul was vulnerable to a neighbouring outbreak, had sent Parker to the city along with the latest team of medics. If the worst happened – which it mostly did, nowadays – then she would need to ensure the safety of local citizens while also stopping Black from spreading beyond the city borders. Parker hadn't even had a chance to set up an office before the harbinger was proved true.

EACH SOLAR PANEL AT PARKER'S TREATMENT CAMP GENERATES A CERTAIN AMOUNT OF ENERGY. HOW MUCH DOES THE LAST ONE GENERATE?

02.06V 01.06V 02.20V 03.24V 02.25V ?

94

News of the Karachi epidemic reached her while she was touring a makeshift treatment camp in some exhibition centre in Şişli. Now she was going to have to hold back a flood using a mobile phone and a couple of maps.

NOTES

10.35

28 Mar

CHECK TENT AND SECURE
BAG UP HOME CLOTHES
WASH HANDS AND SUIT UP
WIPE DOWN ALL WORK SURFACES
CHECK LOCAL MAP!

97

FOR A **HINT**, TURN TO PAGE **194** • FOR THE **SOLUTION**, TURN TO PAGE **210**

WHEN YOU KNOW WHICH OF THE PLANS WAS THE BEST OPTION, YOU CAN PROCEED...

REMEMBER, A SMART RESEARCHER ALWAYS STARTS WITH THE THREE STAGES OF AN EPIDEMIC: INCREASE. INFECT. INTENSIFY.

PLAN A – CODENAME INS

PLAN B – CODENAME CYP

PLAN C – CODENAME SNY

PLAN D – CODENAME PYI

PLAN E – CODENAME SCI

SOLVE TO PASS

FOR A **HINT**, TURN TO PAGE **194** • FOR THE **SOLUTION**, TURN TO PAGE **210**

CHAPTER 6

RESEARCH STATION

LIMA

The cat hung there above her head, perpetual and nameless, on the lip of disaster. Rachel Lethum glanced up at it from her microscope: a sight so familiar that she barely even perceived it any more. It never fell, never got to where it was going. Where was it going? All she knew is that it had followed her dutifully, from dorm room to lab space to faculty office to here, a research station in Lima. Abandoning her slides, she forced herself to actually see it, as if the image might hold some great clue to her own predicament. But it was just a cat.

HANG IN THERE, BABY!

Copyright 1968. Printed in Cheshire.

It was in fine scientific company, at least. Schrödinger, that quantum sadist, had his ambiguously doomed feline, and this was hers: Lethem's cat, simultaneously plunging to its certain fate and hanging in there, baby. Technically, you'd call it a motivational poster, but if its gifting was ironic, does it still count? And what good is ironic motivation anyway when you only have a few days left to save humanity?

She knew she should have been working. She'd already inventoried every crack in the ceiling, each leaf of the houseplant wilting in the corner.

LETHEM DECIDES TO GIVE HER PLANTS SOME LIQUID FOOD. HOW MUCH FOOD (IN MLS) DOES SHE NEED?

FOR A **HINT**, TURN TO PAGE **194** • FOR THE **SOLUTION**, TURN TO PAGE **211**

Her keyboard had never been cleaner. Maybe she could drop chemistry entirely and vie for the Nobel Prize for Procrastination instead. Her university friends used to tease her for exercises in dawdling – her fabled habit of studying the hour hand of her wall clock on its long, slow transit. Certainly, if she spent as much time staring down a microscope, she'd at least be able to afford a new poster.

LETHEM'S MICROSCOPE HAS SOME PRE-SET MAGNIFICATIONS ON IT.

WHICH IS THE MISSING ONE?

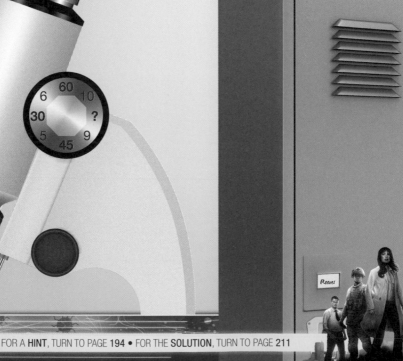

60 10
6
30 ?
5 9
45

FOR A **HINT**, TURN TO PAGE 194 • FOR THE **SOLUTION**, TURN TO PAGE 211

ALL OF THE LIMA TEAM ARE TERRIBLE AT REMEMBERING THEIR THREE-DIGIT LOCKER CODES. WHAT IS LETHEM'S?

Locker Codes Reminders

Reeves	?	+	?	−	3	=	10
	−		+		−		
Lethem	6	−	?	+	?	=	−2
	+		−		+		
Voss	7	−	?	+	?	=	9
	=		=		=		
	9		14		4		

Something was holding her back. It wasn't just the complexity of the assignment or the countless lives depending upon it: there was a gnawing sensation in the pit of her stomach that told her she was about to learn something dangerous.

• • • •

FOR A **HINT**, TURN TO PAGE 194 • FOR THE **SOLUTION**, TURN TO PAGE 211

The only item in the office that Lethem hadn't meticulously catalogued was the one demanding her attention: the teetering stack of case files, sent by her old colleague Margo Lessing. Her job had made her alive to the smallest anomalies – in science, a rogue digit might portend a monumental breakthrough – and this experience had been nothing but anomalies. Why didn't Margo just upload the data to their shared storage? Why hadn't she responded to any emails? Why had they stopped answering the phone at her research station?

Dearest Rachel,

Greetings from sunny Khartoum! I hope Lima is treating you well and that you're keeping out of trouble. The past few months have been wild here, but everyone is pulling together. It's inspiring, truly, despite the inevitable communication difficulties of such a vast international effort. I'm looking forward to the day we can sit in a dusty bar someplace and swap war stories, ideally with Sylvie and Oscar if anyone can tempt them back from Essen!

Sadly, we still haven't found the one cocktail that might best this dreadful malady, but I remain more optimistic than I've ever been. Ahem. Hopefully this will give you a small insight into the work we've been doing here. It's a starting place, at least!

When did you last leave the lab? I must confess I've been part of the "Sleeping Bag Club" for weeks now. I missed August entirely. As far as I'm aware, the finest restaurant in Sudan is the vending machine at the end of the hall. The mountains here are beautiful, though – it reminds me of that summer in Andalusia when we climbed Mulhacén in the Sierra Nevada, quizzing each other on the International Code of Signals the whole way up. We used to feel so aggrieved for living in uninteresting times! Answered prayers, and all that.

Oh well, you can never go home again, as Ella Winter said. These days, I romanticize my terrible haircut and beaten-up Alfa Romero and those frigid November treks to the Stephenson Building, but I'd much rather be here, climbing a different sort of mountain. I do miss you, though. As pleasant as my co-workers are, I don't think any of them have even heard of Contract Whist. Heck, even if I did get out for an afternoon, who could I hit the links.

Bother. I need to send this right now. But you get the idea? Sorry, it's so busy here and the weather is *treacherous*, ha ha.

Love,

Margo X

Even the letter included with the files seemed "off" somehow. Margo was a brilliant researcher but a world-class grumbler, capable of tirades that would make you weep with laughter. Lethem didn't recognize the person in the letter. It certainly wasn't the woman she'd known since university.

Margo had even sent some random bus tickets, presumably intended to go to Payroll along with an expenses claim form, as well as the classic dispatcher map that was used to co-ordinate the movement of medics, researchers and other key personnel to outbreak regions. The test subject results weren't even complete, so there was no way of knowing whether any of the potential cures produced the vital antibodies. It felt as if Margo had been paying no attention at all, but that just didn't seem like her. It wasn't a letter, there were elisions in the letter. But why?

tickets x6

map

Rachel,
For sorting.
Margo x

109

FOR A **HINT**, TURN TO PAGE **195** • FOR THE **SOLUTION**, TURN TO PAGE **212**

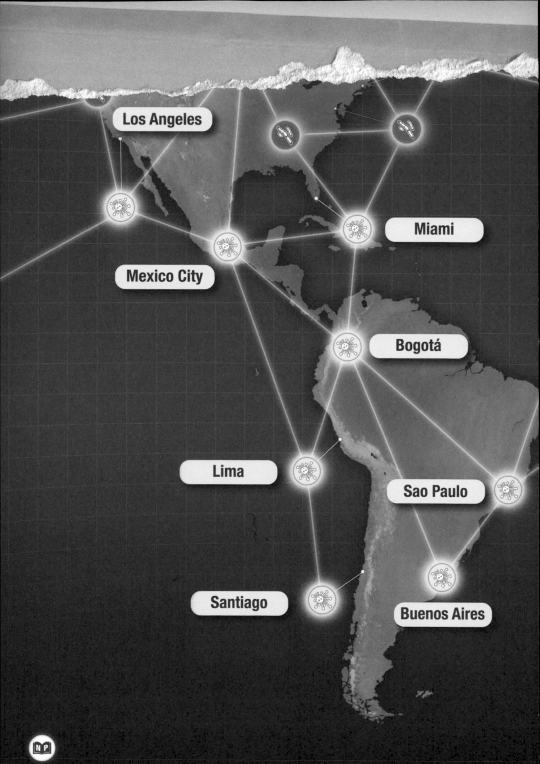

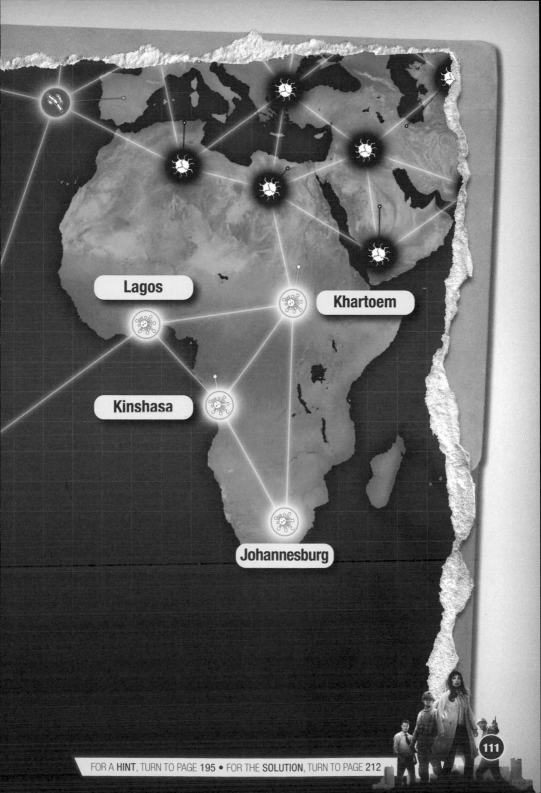

Lagos

Khartoem

Kinshasa

Johannesburg

FOR A **HINT**, TURN TO PAGE **195** • FOR THE **SOLUTION**, TURN TO PAGE **212**

Test Subject Results (Batch 149)

Case no.	Name	Age	D.O.B.	Location	Cocktail given	Antibodies?
157216	P. Martinez	44	28th June	Santiago	CPEAQ-14	...
120352	M. Ntumba	30	13th October	Kinshasa	VSOzP-14	...
189309	R. Miller	25	8th February	Los Angeles	aoFCT-14	...
104728	P. Soares	39	22nd December	São Paulo	NGXal-14	...
191003	A. Umar	51	7th May	Lagos	xVafe-14	...
118492	L. Torres	28	20th January	Mexico City	oYDef-14	...
142831	M. Osman	36	31st July	Khartoum	yslrP-14	...
200240	A. Gomez	27	19th April	Bogotá	ajOge-14	...
220278	J. Quispe	49	3rd August	Lima	LGouY-14	...
157362	D. Jacobs	25	30th June	Johannesburg	XmVAU-14	...
219085	E. Brown	48	13th January	Miami	wbLHy-14	...
134724	H. Nuñez	35	25th March	Buenos Aires	laqUE-14	...

KHARTOUM BUS COMPANY
FROM: University of Khartoum, Epidemic Public Health Institute
TO: Omdurman
Adult single, SDG4.50
BUS 9480
ISSUED ON: 17th August, 2:45
DRIVER 89352

KHARTOUM BUS COMPANY
FROM: University of Khartoum, Epidemic Public Health Institute
TO: Omdurman
Adult single, SDG4.50
BUS 9480
DRIVER 89352
ISSUED ON: 16th August, 3:40

KHARTOUM BUS COMPANY
FROM: University of Khartoum, Epidemic Public Health Institute
TO: Omdurman
Adult single, SDG4.50
BUS 9480
ISSUED ON: 20th August, 1:50
DRIVER 89352

KHARTOUM BUS COMPANY

ISSUED ON: 21st August, 4:30

KHARTOUM BUS COMPANY

FROM: University of Khartoum, Epidemic Public Health Institute

TO: Omdurman

BUS 9480

DRIVER 89352

ISSUED ON: 19th August, 4:25

KHARTOUM BUS COMPANY

FROM: University of Khartoum, Epidemic Public Health Institute

TO: Omdurman

BUS 9480

Adult single, SDG4.50

DRIVER 89352

Test Subject Results (Batch 150)

Case no.	Name	Age	D.O.B.	Location	Cocktail given	Antibodies?
172458	E. Mahlangu	37	13th March	Johannesburg	sjPUR-32	...
127914	B. Sani	46	10th December	Lagos	YaHce-32	...
163892	R. Muñoz	24	10th July	Bogotá	ekHYX-32	...
219448	S. Taha	30	3rd August	Khartoum	lkWwf-32	...
158202	A. Reyes	23	5th May	Santiago	NOJzq-32	...
184058	C. Rojas	46	24th September	Lima	Ljmtx-32	...
148621	U. Perez	43	8th March	Los Angeles	AxfNl-32	...
182745	R. Sosa	39	20th February	Buenos Aires	nwGsy-32	...
113492	J. Gutierrez	50	1st November	Mexico City	xUyCa-32	...
209578	F. Ngoy	44	26th October	Kinshasa	QzjFI-32	...
138460	L. Alves	29	17th April	São Paulo	PUjwG-32	...
192833	S. Wilson	38	4th June	Miami	CMvXn-32	...

ISSUED ON: 18th August, 6:10

KHARTOUM BUS COMPANY

FROM: University of Khartoum, Epidemic Public Health Institute

TO: Omdurman

BUS 9480

Adult single, SDG4.50

DRIVER 89352

113

FOR A **HINT**, TURN TO PAGE 195 • FOR THE **SOLUTION**, TURN TO PAGE 212

Rachel Lethem had never been especially given to apocalyptic thinking – she was a scientist, after all – but she could appreciate the global significance of failing at her task. There was something she found undeniably amusing though – even comforting – about how weirdly mundane her situation was. Two and a half thousand years of medical research, on a genius-strewn path from the four humours to biotechnological companies developing cures using the genetic code of a pathogen, had led to this moment: a tired scientist poring through jumbled materials in the basement of a hastily built lab in Peru, beneath the distracted gaze of a long-retired cat. Somehow fate had rested its hand on her shoulder then gone off for a snack. She took a deep breath and got to work.

WERE ANY OF THE POTENTIAL CURES SUCCESSFUL? ONCE LETHEM HAS TAKEN THE DIFFERENT STEPS TO FIGURE THIS OUT – USING ALL OF THE ELEMENTS AT HER DISPOSAL – YOU CAN PROCEED.

SOLVE TO PASS

NEVER GIVE UP

Copyright 1968. Printed in Cheshire

FOR A **HINT**, TURN TO PAGE **195** • FOR THE **SOLUTION**, TURN TO PAGE **212**

QUARANTINE ZONE

KOLKATA

A deep human dread arises when you find yourself heading in the wrong direction to everyone else. As the truck barrelled down the deserted expressway, Rina Desai couldn't help but stare at the traffic jam blocking the opposing lane.

Desai was reminded of a short story she once read where the protagonist was running away from monstrous birds, only to encounter people running towards the equally terrified birds but by something unknown.

FOR A **HINT**, TURN TO PAGE **195** • FOR THE **SOLUTION**, TURN TO PAGE **214**

Of course, now that the Quarantine Zone covered the entire city, those motorists weren't going to get much closer to Desai's figurative birds anyway. A city of Kolkata's scale is inherently porous, but the port and every significant road were blockaded, and even if someone could get out, there wasn't really anywhere for them to go – the current epidemic had been accelerated by outbreaks in Delhi and Chennai, enveloping the country in days.

Stuck in their "fallen" city, a doomy sort of fatalism had taken hold. Before anybody could move on, they first had to decide which road they should they take next. While there was a sense that Blue and the recently-cured Yellow were finally on the run, Black seemed unstoppable. Expecting a third miracle was almost impolite.

←दानकुनी 14 किमी
DANKUNI 14KM

↑बैरकपुर 17 किमी
BARRACKPORE 17KM

↑चनिसुराह 25 किमी
CHINSURAH 25KM

←हावड़ा 7 किमी
HOWRAH 7KM

121

FOR A **HINT**, TURN TO PAGE **195** • FOR THE **SOLUTION**, TURN TO PAGE **214**

Every setback only served as further confirmation of their collective bad luck; the driver shook his head and huffed as the truck spluttered, its warning lights aglow. Desai could imagine that the truck had been used continually since the crisis began, stopping only for refueling and to let people on and off. Maintenance was a luxury of peacetime, after all, left behind in this era of the quick fix. She pulled the manual out from the side door without needing to be asked.

She refused to believe that a delay was inevitable, but given the blockades and increasing number of vehicles on the road, she'd need to be smart. The road sign they'd passed earlier gave some options for a route into the city, but figuring out the best way of avoiding problems and getting there in one piece would require all of the information at her disposal.

SERIAL NUMBER: FCN-08

INFORMATION LIGHTS

All lights will be illuminated at all times unless the bulb has failed. In this case, you can determine what the colours of the Information Lights mean through the following instructions:

▶ The first of the three bulbs will be illuminated in blue, red, green or yellow, depending on the number of lights of the colours on the dashboard. This bulb will illuminate the same colour that appears the most in other lights on the dashboard, excluding other Information Light bulbs.

20

▶ The second bulb will be illuminated in blue, red, green or yellow, in the colour that appears the least in other lights on the dashboard, excluding other Information Light bulbs.

▶ The final bulb will be lit, but not in the same colour as any other Information Lights. If the total number of the two colours left is odd, the colour that is shown by an odd number of lights is the correct one for this bulb. If the total number is even, the serial number on the dashboard should give an indication of the correct colour.

FOR A **HINT**, TURN TO PAGE **195** • FOR THE **SOLUTION**, TURN TO PAGE **214**

CHAPTER 7: QUARANTINE ZONE, KOLKATA

AS DESAI CAME OFF THE EXPRESSWAY AND INTO A BUSY KOLKATA HIGH STREET, SHE WAS REMINDED OF A RIDDLE THAT USED TO PUZZLE HER AS A CHILD.

IF ROHIN'S SON IS MY SON'S FATHER, THEN WHAT IS MY RELATIONSHIP TO ROHIN?

A) HIS FATHER
B) HIS GRANDFATHER
C) I AM ROHIN
D) HIS SON
E) HIS GRANDSON

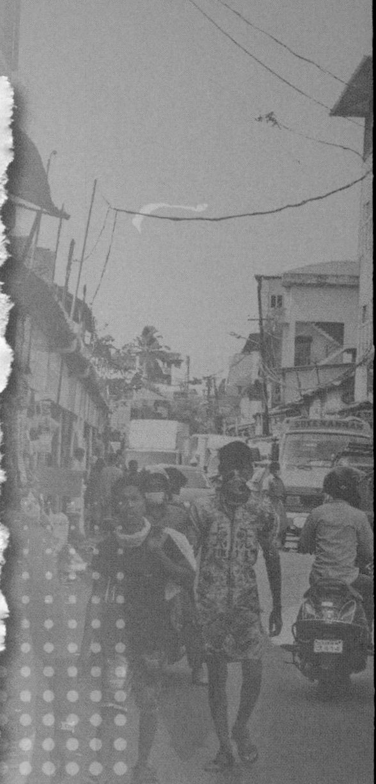

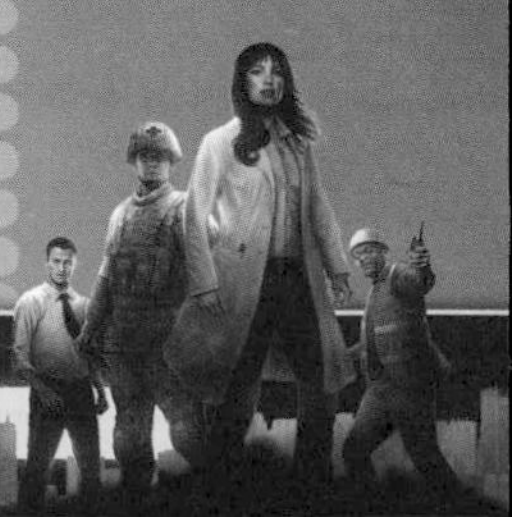

FOR A **HINT**, TURN TO PAGE 195 • FOR THE **SOLUTION**, TURN TO PAGE 214

It wasn't the return she'd envisioned. Desai's research had brought her into the orbit of the Global Health Agency – most significant virologists eventually submitted to its gravitational pull – but Kolkata was her home town, or at least as much of a home town as a city with 14 million residents (in its greater metropolitan area) can be. While she'd witnessed Black's path of destruction from Algiers to Moscow, it was crushing to see it happen here. From the genome level to its continental sweep, she'd seen more of the virus than almost anyone, yet a subterranean part of her had also believed, in the face of all reason, that it somehow hadn't touched her home. It had done worse than that: at this moment, Kolkata was the white-hot epicentre of the pandemic, the most perilous spot on the map, and she was heading straight into it.

5

6

• • • •

The truck pulled up to the hospital. Desai clambered out, obscurely concerned that she would see someone she knew. It didn't seem like the kind of thing that should happen given the size of the city, yet she dependably ran into an old colleague or a friend of her auntie every time she visited. On this occasion, however, the circumstances of a chance meeting would be grave.

For a summer in her childhood, Desai had flirted with the idea of becoming an astronaut, but other than that, this was the most ambitious goal she'd ever set herself. She'd arrived into Kolkata determined to vanquish Black. The details of Yellow's cure were still strangely opaque, but like Blue, it appeared that the breakthrough came from direct analysis of stricken patients concentrated in a heavily affected area. Although the diseases themselves differed on almost every level, their simultaneous emergence suggested some commonality in how their cures could be approached. She had to try, even if it meant compromising her own safety.

You could always tell a new ward: Desai set herself up in a tertiary care unit that was about to be opened just before the pandemic had struck. A range of patients for her to take specimens from had been brought in that morning.

DESAI WALKED INTO THE WARD, AND TRIED TO FIND A SPARE DESK TO SET UP AT.

She was somewhat superstitious, and only wanted to sit in a room with an "even" amount of desks. She wanted to see Kolkata, so made sure she was in a room with a balcony.

She was cautious, and wanted to be in a room close to a fire escape.

She liked plants, so wanted to make sure she was in a room with a plant.

She didn't like people walking past too often, so she wanted to sit as far away from the door as she could.

Desai didn't want to sit behind a desk where the whole number was "odd".

She liked the idea of sitting directly behind a desk number whose last digit was a multiple of its first digit.

WHICH DESK WAS HERS?

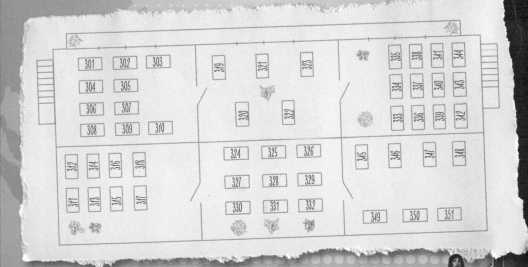

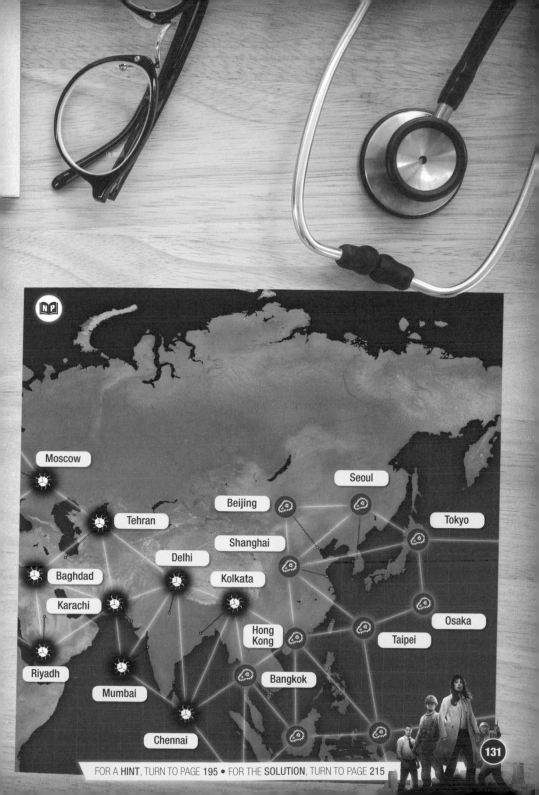

FOR A **HINT**, TURN TO PAGE 195 • FOR THE **SOLUTION**, TURN TO PAGE 215

FOR A **HINT**, TURN TO PAGE 195 • FOR THE **SOLUTION**, TURN TO PAGE 215

Desai liked hard work – she could barely imagine life without it – but this was less straightforward that she'd been expecting. Results had come in from various cities, and apparently one of the test subjects had successfully produced antibodies, but information was missing. Even the city that provided the success was unclear, the data fractured.

3   7

FROM: @*%£$£@&

TO: R*n& Des)i

Rina, I'm having trouble gett*ng emai£ through. They seem to @£& corrupt£d as I send. We have a success. Our patient, case number (@1^£# has shown antibodies. It won't e*@n let me send case numbers. Let me try this.

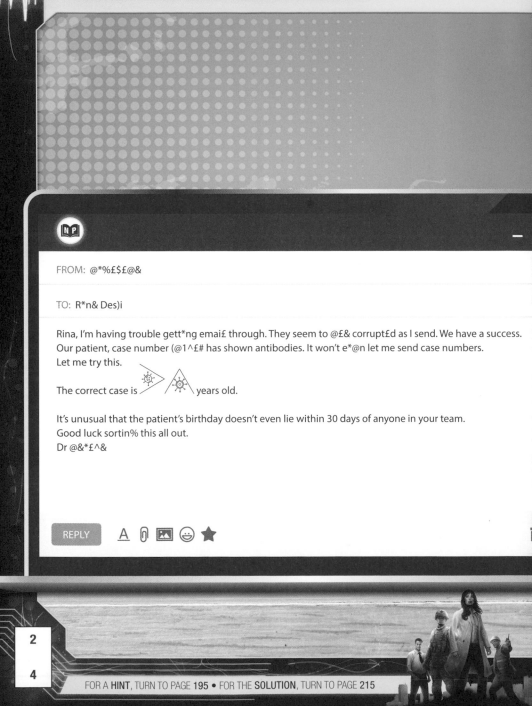

The correct case is ⟩⟩ years old.

It's unusual that the patient's birthday doesn't even lie within 30 days of anyone in your team.
Good luck sortin% this all out.
Dr @&*£^&

REPLY A 📎 🖼 😊 ⭐

2

4

FOR A **HINT**, TURN TO PAGE 195 • FOR THE **SOLUTION**, TURN TO PAGE 215

The whole email was suspicious, especially the sentence about the subject's birthday. It was like an affectation of a corrupted message. Why did this information need to be hidden? If the whispers from her distant colleagues were correct, this was beginning to become a habit. Desai gathered the ID cards of her team, hoping to find the one test subject that had been given the successful cocktail.

Name: **P. Thakur**

DoB: **1st February**

Name: **F. Das**

DoB: **7th April**

Name: **B. Chand**

DoB: **8th November**

Name: **R. Desai**

DoB: **18th January**

Name: **E. Solanki**

DoB: **13th May**

Name: **T. Chaudhary**

DoB: **28th July**

FOR A **HINT**, TURN TO PAGE **195** • FOR THE **SOLUTION**, TURN TO PAGE **215**

Test Subject Results (Batch 185)

Case no.	Name	Age	D.O.B.	Location	Cocktail given	Antibodies?
391262	J. Ram	36	15th December	Delhi	BKlPw-18	...
316601	P. Kumar	58	9th June	Chennai	MWWkP-18	...
361296	E. Yadav	25	28th February	Kolkata	FgceT-18	...
301105	N. Ali	34	12th February	Delhi	rYDmK-18	...
321234	G. Singh	42	30th December	Mombai	CBIMb-18	...
351034	W. Sharma	52	18th June	Kolkata	fEMkk-18	...
371015	R. Mondal	37	1st September	Mombai	pTcLv-18	...
401175	L. Khan	34	4th March	Delhi	bBoSD-18	...
389071	D. Kumari	40	15th April	Kolkata	LaMIL-18	...
351773	H. Patil	27	5th March	Mombai	cYpHS-18	...
362518	R. Ansari	52	23rd June	Chennai	EqVnm-18	...
351257	A. Prasad	36	1st April	Delhi	yNASW-18	...

SOLVE TO PASS

CHAPTER 8

GLOBAL HEALTH AGENCY

LA CONFLUENCE

It was unproductive to ascribe motivation to infectious diseases, but sometimes it felt like the pandemic was deliberately punishing Georges Rosenthal for feeling hope. Each apparent success just demonstrated how many more successes were needed. The end kept getting further away, like the paradox where Achilles never overtakes the tortoise because it's always moving forward.

And yet, with Blue, Yellow and now Black cured and waning, perhaps the end – or the closest to an end that one could reasonably hope for – was finally in view. A tortoise couldn't keep trudging forever, surely. This optimism was shared by Rosenthal's colleagues. Lately, he'd noticed that they'd started to unselfconsciously refer to long-term plans – house moves, starting families – in a way that had seemed improper before. Discarding all recent evidence, the future was something they were allowing themselves to believe in again – as a place they might return to.

I can't wait to go see Racing 92 – Powell

Not Lyon?? Traitor! As soon as this is over I'm moving out of my shoebox – Carter

Escape Room, anyone? – Duggan

I miss browsing the shops! – Soutar

A bar for me... Any bar, as long as it serves craft beer and wings – Morton

This lasted as long as he might have expected. A cloud moved in front of the sun and then it was overcast again. Another chain reaction meant Red was spiking across Southeast Asia, as if aggrieved by the progress made elsewhere. Of the hundreds of staff at the La Confluence Institute in Lyon – technically the GHA's main headquarters, although the importance of Atlanta's Dispatcher Response Unit had muddied the waters somewhat – it was Rosenthal who was inevitably contacted when things went wrong. He was contacted a lot. In an earlier age, he would have required a dedicated switchboard operator; he'd somehow made and received half a dozen calls between exiting his car and swiping his identification card to enter the building.

ROSENTHAL WAS ALWAYS MAKING CALLS, BUT THE ONE NUMBER HE NEVER REMEMBERED WAS HIS OWN. HE DOODLED A REMINDER ON THE BACK OF HIS PHONE.

WHAT IS HIS EIGHT-DIGIT TELEPHONE NUMBER?

FOR A **HINT**, TURN TO PAGE 195 • FOR THE **SOLUTION**, TURN TO PAGE 216

ROSENTHAL STORES HIS MOST IMPORTANT NOTES IN HIS BRIEFCASE, BUT IT IS LOCKED WITH TWO FOUR-DIGIT CODES. HE LEAVES IT AT 0000-0000, SO THE CODE CANNOT BE THAT, BUT HE KEEPS A REMINDER ON HIS COFFEE MUG.

WHAT ARE THE TWO CODES?

FOR A **HINT**, TURN TO PAGE 195 • FOR THE **SOLUTION**, TURN TO PAGE 216

As Contingency Planner, Rosenthal was expected to plot a new direction when catastrophe struck. His job had never been more necessary. For all the optimism going around, global infection rates were dangerously high. Even at this late stage, there was a tipping point at which the devastation would be irreversible. A "lose state" was the most euphemistic way he could think to describe what would be an unprecedented outcome, resembling some of the spicier sections of various holy books.

There was something else, too. A four-headed global pandemic was challenging beyond measure, but he'd become convinced that there was also another force at work. Although he first became aware of it when he received a call from a panicked Operations Expert in Ho Chi Minh City, he suspected it had been going on far longer. Someone had been undermining their work at every turn. This went beyond deadly construction sites or failing systems. The research station in Khartoum had never returned from its radio silence. It had disappeared from satellite imagery entirely. Its staff had vanished, *actually vanished*, in the twenty-first century. It was as if they had never existed. The coordinated nature of these obstacles meant only one thing: *A person working within the GHA was responsible.*

Rosenthal hadn't spoken to anyone about his suspicions. Even when colleagues – a Researcher in Lima, Troubleshooter Sophie Shepherd in Atlanta – had confidentially expressed their concerns, he'd discouraged the notion that anything was awry. If there really was a Bio-Terrorist at work, they needed to believe that they were completely undetected. If there had been any lesson to take from the pandemic, it was that people thought they were strongest when they were truly at their most vulnerable.

Clearly there was a great French detective in him, waiting to get out. Rosenthal met the gaze of every colleague he passed in the hallway. They just seemed like normal people. He'd bought them drinks on their birthdays, asked after their children, eaten the home-made *canistrelli* and *chouquettes* they'd brought in. The idea that one of them had been actively working against the team's efforts deeply saddened him. He was so proud of the work they'd done together. It was perhaps the most meaningful thing any of them would ever do. They'd missed months of their lives in service of the health of strangers – and now this.

ONE OF ROSENTHAL'S COLLEAGUES, REGAN, WAS TALKING ABOUT HIS CHILDREN'S LATEST EXTRACURRICULAR ACTIVITIES AND MENTIONED THAT HIS "TAP DANCE SUPERSTAR" WOULD BE ARRIVING SHORTLY FOR A VISIT.

Even though he'd met the four children many times, and knew their names. Rosenthal could not remember which one was which. He tried to pay close attention to Regan's story, to remember who was who.

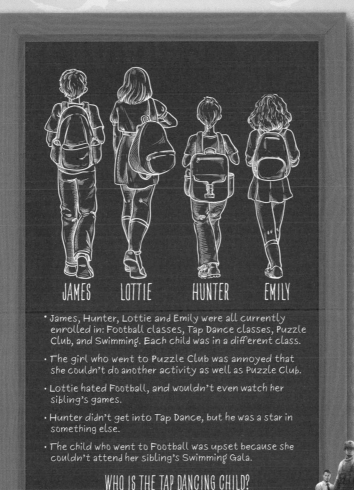

JAMES   LOTTIE   HUNTER   EMILY

- James, Hunter, Lottie and Emily were all currently enrolled in: Football classes, Tap Dance classes, Puzzle Club, and Swimming. Each child was in a different class.

- The girl who went to Puzzle Club was annoyed that she couldn't do another activity as well as Puzzle Club.

- Lottie hated Football, and wouldn't even watch her sibling's games.

- Hunter didn't get into Tap Dance, but he was a star in something else.

- The child who went to Football was upset because she couldn't attend her sibling's Swimming Gala.

WHO IS THE TAP DANCING CHILD?

FOR A **HINT**, TURN TO PAGE 196 • FOR THE **SOLUTION**, TURN TO PAGE 216

Rosenthal suppressed a sigh, remembering the best advice he'd ever been given: think about the process, not the outcome. His diving coach at high school had said it about his somersault pike, but experience had taught him that it applied to just about anything. He needed to focus on the task at hand and leave the sorrow for another day. He'd already figured out that the access logs would lead him to the person who'd been hiding the test result data and corrupting internal emails – the Bio-Terrorist – but his attempts to retrieve them had led to an error message. At first he'd assumed this was a dead end, but he let his eyes adjust to the dark, and saw the glint of a handle.

```
>Load Access Logs
LOCKED FILE - ACCESS DENIED.
>Load Locked File Signature

LAST USED KEY SIGNATURE:


R  R  R  D  D  L  L  U  L  U
L  U  R  U  R  D  D  D  L  U
D  L  D  L  U  U  U  R  D  R
R  R  R  D  L  D  L  L  U  U
D  R  U  U  L  L  L  D  R  R
D  L  D  R  R  U  U  L


S  I  B  L  N  Z  C  Y  G  T  E  J  U  W  R  H  D  K  M  X  O  F  P  A  Q  V
26 16  8  3 20 14 22  6  1 14 13  7 18 11 10 21  5  9 23 15 17 12  2 24 25  4
```

FOR A **HINT**, TURN TO PAGE **196** • FOR THE **SOLUTION**, TURN TO PAGE **217**

The Bio-Terrorist had finally over-extended themselves and they didn't even know it. By trying to block him, they'd left themselves unguarded. Whoever had locked access to the file would be the one he'd been looking for, so he just needed to decipher their key signature to identify them. It wasn't a dead end, after all. It was the way out.

SOLVE TO PASS

CHAPTER 9

HOSPITAL
JAKARTA

As his men removed the nets from the tennis courts of the Shangri-La Hotel, Luca Shapton was thinking about Saigon again. While those government employees on the roof of 22 Gia Long Street, waiting to squeeze on to a too-small helicopter, had become the definitive symbol of American misadventure in the Vietnam War, the image itself was not unique. Over the decades, similar scenes punctuated the end of other hapless conflicts. You could probably trace the notion back to Dunkirk, that original miracle of British queueing, but its meaning had evolved as the scenario lingered in the public imagination. An emergency airlift always felt like a failure, saved lives overshadowed by their embodiment of a retreat in action.

This was what both Shapton's therapist and his former partner would call "unhelpful thinking". As coordinated by himself and other Field Operatives, heavy-lift helicopters would soon be landing to collect the district's remaining population and create a firewall around the quarantine zone. It wasn't a defeat – the pandemic wasn't an opposing army, despite the rhetoric – it was a public health measure to protect much of north-west Java. But it felt like a defeat, so what was the difference, really? Every day, the news showed the three diseases being beaten back in Africa, Europe, India, South America – and yet every day another city fell to Red. A thousand miles north of Jakarta, were there people in Ho Chi Minh City queueing on a similiar roof?

SHAPTON LOOKED AT THE WIND DIRECTION AND WEATHER REPORT FOR THE HELICOPTERS, KNOWING THAT WE ARE LIVING IN UNUSUAL TIMES. WHAT TEMPERATURE WILL IT BE IN THE EVENING IN JAKARTA?

FOR A **HINT**, TURN TO PAGE 196 • FOR THE **SOLUTION**, TURN TO PAGE 218

Shapton corrected himself. Every day another city endured Red. The Global Health Agency had agreed to stop using the expression "fallen", fearing perceptions of the afflicted regions that would fester for years after the pandemic had ended – not to mention the fact that there were so many of them now that it would be problematic (and rude) to describe entire countries as fallen. Still, if the term could be applied with accuracy anywhere, it would be Jakarta. It was enduring Red, all right. From the very beginning, the city had been hit by wave upon wave of Red, and even outbreaks of Black for a stretch. The resilience of the people never wavered; it made no difference.

He could hear the helicopters now. They couldn't come soon enough – the evacuees had been amassing since before dawn. Shapton checked his plans again and again, as if they might have washed off the page whenever he looked up. He'd also been told that this form of apprehension was unhelpful, but he disagreed. Anxiety was paralyzing until it wasn't. If you used it correctly, anxiety brought the world into focus, dilating time itself. This was only one part of the story, of course, but it would do until he'd gotten those evacuees to safety.

Think about the process and not the outcome

FOR A **HINT**, TURN TO PAGE **196** • FOR THE **SOLUTION**, TURN TO PAGE **218**

Shapton watched the helicopters until he could no longer see them; after they were out of sight, he watched the space where they'd once been. Every person who'd stepped on board would have considered it an unquestionable good – and who was he to argue? These days, you took victory where you could get it.

A van took him and his men back to the hospital. When he'd first flown into the city, the original intention had been to keep the building quarantined, an order which had since come under scrutiny. Shapton had no idea exactly what was going on at the GHA, but messages from a few colleagues suggested that they'd been some kind of major arrest. Embezzlement, maybe? There always seemed to be well-connected people who became richer during pandemics while contracts mysteriously flowed in their direction. What this had to do with a mid-sized hospital in Jakarta was unclear. In any case, all patients except for those on the Red wards would be moved and processed.

THE STAFF UNIFORMS ALL HAVE A BADGE THAT IS RELATED TO AN ID NUMBER.

WHICH NUMBER MATCHES EACH BADGE?

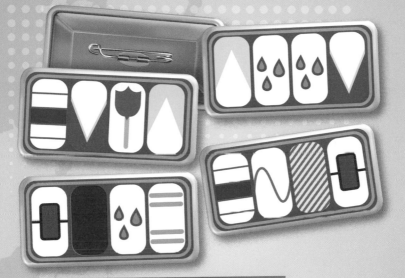

STAFF IDs

1504
1976
4328
6229

CHAPTER 9: HOSPITAL, JAKARTA

Upon his arrival, Shapton was told that a patient wanted to see him. A relative of an evacuee, perhaps, looking for reassurance that they'd gotten out okay. He was surprised to find an American woman, alone in a ward, fidgeting on a cot. She seemed relieved and irritated in equal proportion. He suspected that the latter condition was permanent.

The ward itself seemed fairly routine except for a collection of patient lockers along one wall, elaborately secured. If the patients were right there, why you need to padlock their stuff? A chain of ten keys hung just out of reach of the perturbed woman – the extra key, evidently, destined for her own locker.

FOR A **HINT**, TURN TO PAGE **196** • FOR THE **SOLUTION**, TURN TO PAGE **219**

"Mr Shapton, hello," she said, the IV drip catching her before she could offer her hand.

"My name is Margo Lessing. I need you to fly me out of Jakarta right now, ideally without this lousy bed."

She presented Shapton with her ID card. Perhaps this would tell him where she needed to go. Once he'd figured out where that was, he liberated her personal effects from her locker.

Margo Lessing
Scientist

FOR A **HINT**, TURN TO PAGE 196 • FOR THE **SOLUTION**, TURN TO PAGE 219

SNACK PLAN FOR HOPPER

HOPPER

Hopper can have one of each of these treats:
Cheese, Biscuit, Carrot, Meat, Apple, Peanut Butter

To prevent tummy upset, they can only be given in this order:

- Carrot can only be given sometime after Apple
- Meat should never be given directly before or after Cheese, Biscuit, Apple or Peanut Butter
- Apple should only be given sometime before Biscuit
- Peanut Butter can only be given sometime between Cheese and Carrot
- Biscuit should only be given sometime before Cheese

SOLVE TO PASS

BEFORE SHAPTON CAN LEAVE, HE NEEDED TO MAKE SURE THAT HIS DOG-SITTER KNEW WHAT TO FEED HIS DOG, HOPPER.

IN WHAT ORDER CAN THE TREATS BE GIVEN?

169

FOR A **HINT**, TURN TO PAGE **196** • FOR THE **SOLUTION**, TURN TO PAGE **219**

CHAPTER 10

DISPATCHER RESPONSE UNIT

ATLANTA

Was it a geopolitical manoeuvre? Did he have ideological reasons? Had it all just been about money? Although the Bio-Terrorist's identity was now known, his motivations remained opaque. He sat in his cell, refusing to speak; a void replaced by another void. The sabotage had been clearly plotted to cause maximum disruption, appearing random enough to be unnoticed amid a world in upheaval. There was no apparent link between the origin of the diseases and his efforts, but he'd been poised to take full advantage of them.

"Why?" was, thankfully, a question for other people to solve. It did seem, at least for now, that he worked alone – of course, when you followed the trail back far enough, even lone wolves usually seemed to be funded by some "respectable" institution. If he did represent other parties, they had now been presumably thwarted, if not wholly eliminated. This didn't make anyone feel better.

Theoretically, those at the GHA who'd suspected treachery could be relieved. Sophie Shepherd counted herself among that number; she wasn't relieved. She did feel proud of Georges Rosenthal in La Confluence for figuring out the whole thing, but her disquiet stuck. Even disregarding the global outcry that was surely coming their way, the damage had been done, and at the worst possible time. Red was unstoppable. The cures weren't enough. Even with Blue, Yellow and Black cured, infection rates were at a historic peak. It was never a good sign when you started receiving company-wide emails instructing everyone to avoid saying "the point of no return".

Shepherd stared at the map in her office. It had been put up by her Bio-Terrorist predecessor, a fact that she hadn't even realized until his capture reminded her of the envelope in her drawer. By now the map was so out-of-date that it may as well have included Uruk, Byzantium and Siam. She kept it up as a reminder that – actually, she didn't know why she kept it up. Perhaps she was just superstitious, remembering her first day when she and Shōnagon had, improbably, saved the people of Essen.

FROM: B. Samwell

TO: All

Dear all,

The other heads of departments and I have decided that the terminology in use risks causing psychological and further economic damage. As you are aware, should the general population become disheartened, or feel hopeless, our job becomes exponentially more difficult. Because of this we request that you cease using the term "the point of no return", instead replacing it with less final terms, such as "the next level" or "a concerning increase".

Thank you for your continued exceptional work.

B. Samwell

Encryption Key

•<<EMBARL4NA9LCQMK2N1JC•

•PSWLKH1ZIM5TK0EXE2R3•

•SGRKEEBVD4J4EA•

•SDB3HL7HUVBE2M8DX>>•

REPLY

Black

Yellow

Grey

White

SHEPHERD'S DESK WAS LOCKED SHUT – BUT NONE OF
THE KEYS HANGING ON THE WALL OPENED IT. INSTEAD, IT
REQUIRED TWO FOUR-DIGIT CODES.

WHAT WAS THE COMBINATION?

FOR A **HINT**, TURN TO PAGE 196 • FOR THE **SOLUTION**, TURN TO PAGE 220

Maybe there was something comforting about the idea that the pandemic existed on a continuum. It had gotten worse, so it could also get better. She didn't believe in a point of no return: she was a Troubleshooter.

Shepherd's eyes drifted to the edge of the map. There was an air bubble in the South Pacific that she hadn't noticed before. She pushed it in. It sprung back into place. "Here be dragons," she said to herself, while a cartoon lightbulb went off somewhere above her head. She took the map off the wall and turned it over.

There was a note stuck to the back of the map. It was from *him*.

• • • •

404-706-0539

2928 LIMER STREET
ATLANTA, GEORGIA

GHA.2MAN

To my successor,

You are never going to read this message. It is going to sit here, a foot away
your desk, while the world collapses around you. You will never know that the
solution was literally within your grasp, gazing down upon you during all those
long, fruitless months. After you're eventually fired for your incompetence,
shuffling out of the remnants of the disgraced Global Health Assembly, I will
casually pop by my old office — just for old times' sake, I'll say — and remove
this like it was never there at all. I'm pretty sure I will be smiling.

So here is it, then, the information you need. You may have noticed that the GHA
data keeps corrupting upon transfer. This will be my (successful) attempt to slow
you down: a program I've installed on the networked servers. You can deactivate
it — not that that you will, obviously — by decoding your encryption keys, typing
in the following instruction to the command prompt on your machine.

EVERYTHIRDLETTER

Maybe you'll also need that newspaper I left you, but I imagine you threw that
out on your first day. I would pity you, but it's not worth the seconds.

Your faithful colleague,

S

The phone rang. It was Georges Rosenthal to say that a colleague had just reported to work, a few thousand miles removed and several weeks late. He put her on.

"Hello, Ms Shepherd? I'm Margo. I'll be brief because I've just spent a month stranded on a hospital bed in Jakarta. When I arrived at La Confluence, I asked Georges which individual needed this information first. He said you, so here we are. I was working at the Lima Research Station when I discovered the cure for Yellow. It became apparent, however, that one of my co-workers was not working for the same team, let's say. I was able to smuggle my work out to Rachel Lethem before – by astonishing coincidence – every single member of the team came down with Yellow, at the exact same time. We were then scattered to hospitals in fallen cities–"

"Sorry, uh, we don't say 'fallen' any more."

"That's sensible. We were abandoned in quarantined areas, kept in isolated hospital wards 'for our own good'. Or I was, anyway – logic dictates that we all suffered the same fate. Thanks supposedly to our mutual friend, Georges, I was able to escape. All that time did give me an opportunity to run over the data, though."

"You had it all in your head?"

"Just the good bits. I realized something I'd overlooked the first time. Structurally, Blue and Black are siloed, but the Red and Yellow viruses are related. I'd explain how but I'd need a whiteboard and some grant money. It made me wonder if the patients cured from Yellow would also have antibodies against Red. I thought about the documents I'd used all that time ago – perhaps a similar cocktail of drugs could work on both. If I could figure out the missing parts that were lost through the encrypted transfer, I'd determine which cocktail from the Yellow tests would also work on Red. In short: you cure Yellow, you cure Red. And, Ms Shepherd, I cured Yellow."

ily News

ur World. Your News. Now.

LLNESS APPEARS IN JAKARTA

FOR A **HINT**, TURN TO PAGE **196** • FOR THE **SOLUTION**, TURN TO PAGE **221**

Shepherd dropped into the chair next to Shōnagon. It was her favourite spot in the building. She gestured at the bank of monitors.

"What's our problem, pal?"

Shōnagon picked up his train whistle and gave a half-hearted blow.

"Our problem is that we're fighting four diseases at the same time: one of them incurable, all of them relentless."

				BOND	?	
DALE	CHINYERE				AHMED	
	EDWARDS					

"What if that wasn't true?"

"How do you mean?"

"What if Red had been cured?"

Shepherd gripped Shōnagon's arm. His eyebrow climbed a quarter of an inch.

"Has it?"

"It has."

"That's extraordinary news. But we're still in the same situation. We're approaching the point of...the point that an administrative edict has forbidden us to name."

"Yes, but what if, instead of spreading ourselves even further – hear me out – we now direct all of the GHA's resources to eradicating Yellow? As quick as we can, we take it off the board, thus making the other diseases surmountable."

"It would be a wild risk, and you know how I feel about wild risks."

"You love them."

"Exactly."

Cairo

Riyadh

G M

Khartoum

W

L

Kinshasa

E T

Johannesburg

S

185

FOR A **HINT**, TURN TO PAGE 197 • FOR THE **SOLUTION**, TURN TO PAGE 222

CHAPTER 10: DISPATCHER RESPONSE UNIT, ATLANTA

THE ELECTRONICS STORAGE CUPBOARD'S THREE-DIGIT PASSCODE HAS BEEN ENCRYPTED INTO SOME COMPUTER CODE, STORING THE NAMES OF THE GHA'S TEAM LEADERS.

WHAT IS THE PASSCODE?

TEAM LEADERS

Shōnagon
Shepherd
Lessing
Rosenthal
Lethem
Parker
Vowell
Tokarczuk
Shapton
Saunders

```
B L R V C Q T Y U R P A R V Y N U M U S H V R Ö N
J R O S E N T H A L F D Y B T H R I V E S A D E C
N A R E K T R A L D G E X A B T U T M P L O W X S
D F H D H U R E Y F S S C R G V X S G C U Y I E Z
X V E C A C W D S L E T H E M D Y R S X V N J G D
O G E C T O C X H F R B I C Z R X R W V J T V T X
X S I C V X C E Ö X A B C T N E D W Y B M W Z Q P
U D C N Q W N X N K G D K W E H F U E W C B M Z T
O I W J D A A G A M V S E O T P G M X A F H I R Q
A N P L N U B T G S R D N V H E R O N E C Y B X Q
S G C E F B E T O C B M B E R H E R T F D A Z D S
E C R S B N J R N R E K R A P S N O T P A H S K P
E A D F V G R H J I T H D H V D W F G H C D E U S
S W E C A D S I R E N E E S X C H J Y D W C G Z E
E R V C G S L W D D G H J T D S A D H J K L F C W
O X S X S A V F B H N K F T M D O S A U N D E R S
B W E X E L L D K C W F Ö C R X S X V D S X V A Z
Z X P C F C F L A P S C D S C E B S E C G J X K E
L J P B V X D D B H G S S S F H J K K T R V S O D
D E G N B S W W E U B S W G V X L E S S I N G T U
```

FOR A **HINT**, TURN TO PAGE 197 • FOR THE **SOLUTION**, TURN TO PAGE 222

Shōnagon had a way of transforming chaos into its most rational and mundane form, like a hydroelectro dam that takes a mighty river and uses it to power a kettle. His was such a *sensible* superpower that it was invisible to almost everyone except Shepherd. But that was enough for him. By the time she'd returned to the DRU, sandwich in tow, Shōnagon had already plotted out a strategy. He flourished his train whistle as if he was another sort of conductor.

"You'll notice that I've updated the map. It shows the current status of infections, with a visual representation of the severity shown by individual cubes. I've marked these cubes with letters to help us discuss our approach. We have five groups on the ground to deal with the pandemic – the names of each medic are listed. Each group has a certain number of 'movement resources' they can make from their starting point, and each team member in the group can stay behind in a city and handle one cube. In this case, it will only be possible if all cubes in a city are wiped out by one group. A movement resource will allow a group to travel between two adjacent cities. Once we've figured all that out, we'll need to call my Dispatcher counterpart in Lyon to coordinate."

Home   Insert   Draw   Page Layout   Formulas   Data   Review   View   Tell me

	A	B	C	D	E
1	**Medics**	**Current Position**	**Number of Repositions**	**Number of Team Members**	
2					
3	Edwards	Start in Khartoum	2 moves	5 team members	
4	Bond	Start in Khartoum	1 move	4 team members	
5	Ahmed	Start in L.A.	2 moves	5 team members	
6	Dale	Start in Khartoum	2 moves	3 team members	
7	Chinyere	Start in Santiago	3 moves	9 team members	
8					
9					
10					
11					
12					
13					
14					

Shepherd squinted at him. "I assume you don't actually need my help to shoot this particular trouble?"

"No, it's within my operational capacity...I realize that makes me sound like a robot, but it's the clearest way to put it. Given the long road we've been on, I just thought it would be fitting to take these final steps together."

"I hope these aren't our final steps."

"Well, when you've accomplished this, you'll also know the name of the person to call."

"You old charmer, you."

She shook her sandwich in Shōnagon's direction. He was almost smiling.

HINTS

HINTS

PROLOGUE

Page 9

If 7 is next to 1, then 6 must be before 7.

CHAPTER 1

Page 13

Two sets of lines? Or one set across two sides?

Pages 16-19

The building's floors are marked with letters, not numbers.

Pages 20-24

Didn't you see a newspaper recently?

CHAPTER 2

Page 30

Maybe what you can see is what should be missing?

Pages 32-37

The virus' name is a clue to your resources, and some people need to go further than others.

Page 39

You might blow it if you use the letters in the right order.

Page 41

Y+Y+Y must end in either 0 or 5.

CHAPTER 3

Page 46

You can order takeaway from one room to the next.

Pages 48-49

The colour code comes from the people who built it.

Page 51

Their colour indicates the right path to take.

Page 52

You're on the right track if you follow the path.

Page 54

The numbers on the trees match the numbers on the materials.

Page 56-57

These materials are for connection as well as construction.

Page 59

We should underline that each of these snacks has a little bit of what you're seeking.

Pages 62-63

Wood comes from trees, and so does the solution.

CHAPTER 4

Page 66

Red has infected less than Yellow but more than Black.

Page 67

This person is feeling left out, but they need to be.

Page 69

The more cultures there are, the further along you must go.

Page 70-71

Both people and samples can have ages.

Page 73

Neither Gerry nor Lou begins with H.

Page 75

Credit card debts often double in pandemics.

Page 76

Her parents gave her this password, but others have trouble spelling it.

Page 77

Blue isn't just an emotion, it's also a colour for liquids.

Page 79

Try to find who it can't be, either by age, code or name.

CHAPTER 5

Page 82

The fifth line tells you all the colours you need, the rest will show where they are positioned.

Page 83

Look for these letters on the map.

Page 84-85

Follow the path to the graph.

Page 87

The number and colour of what you find on the path will give you the data points you need.

Page 88-89

Bold words in an epidemic often lead to messages.

Page 91

You should still save three of the dates, get the message?

Page 93

There's an epidemic of messages, with a band of three in particular.

Page 94

The more columns and panels, the more energy you have.

Pages 96-97

You can often find band posters in the streets around here.

Page 99

Three words, lead to three messages, lead to three bands, lead to three letters.

CHAPTER 6

Page 102

If this cat disappears, maybe a smile would be left behind.

Page 103

The spider plant must need a third of the first total.

Page 104

Multiplication is the key here.

Page 105

Voss' code has a 0 in the middle.

Page 108
The international code will help find the letters of a starting place, Oscar Kilo?

Pages 112-113
Page Ignore the month, and think about a clock's hands on the map.

CHAPTER 7

Page 119
The cars' days are numbered.

Page 121
You can find your intended destination here.

Page 123
The three colours can lead you into a traffic jam.

Page 124
You're not Rohin.

Page 129
The balcony is at the top, and both rooms either side have fire escape access.

Page 132
It's a capital location on the map.

Page 134
Scattered around this chapter's pages, matching symbols and numbers in places.

Pages 136-137
As the email says, the test subject doesn't have a birthday 30 days before or after any of these people.

CHAPTER 8

Page 141
One these people has greater importance than the others.

Page 143
The path will give you the numbers you seek.

Page 144
The briefcase shows that Heart equals 0.

Page 146-147

With directions you can draw the truth out from these building's shapes.

Page 149

Pay attention to the pronouns in the statements.

Page 151

Up, down, left and right is the key to drawing out these important shapes.

CHAPTER 9

Page 158

Put North at the top and then think about clocks, and how night is the opposite of day…

Page 161

Look to where their destinations cross.

Page 163

Look for where there's a double in the middle.

Pages 166-167

Imagine putting each key in the lock. Would it fit?

Page 168

A stripe on the side will get you in the air.

Page 169

As Meat can only be next to Carrot, it cannot come before anything else.

CHAPTER 10

Page 174

The saboteur's letter holds the key to the key.

Page 175

Look at the colour of the word, and then the word of the colour.

Page 181

1-5 are the groups. Add the numbers of the colours together, and then you can use the code the bioterrorist mentions to find the cure you seek in a past trial.

Page 182

The names on the screens match
the position of the cubes.

Pages 184-185

Once you find their final
destination, the letter will become
clear.

Page 186

The lines of the words show you
the numbers.

Page 188

Each move will allow you to
eliminate a certain number of
cubes, and so you must be as
efficient as possible. Then the
alphabet will help you know
what order the letters you find
must be in.

SOLUTIONS

PROLOGUE

Page 9

The numbers are **6,7,1,9,18**. The code translates this as **VIRUS**.

A	B	C	D	E	F	G	H	I	J	K	L	M	N	O	P	Q	R	S	T	U	V	W	X	Y	Z
12	24	3	16	10	20	21	14	7	19	2	8	15	26	5	11	25	1	18	23	9	6	13	17	5	22

CHAPTER 1

Page 13

Star = **H** Circle = **E** Square = **A** Triangle = **L**

HEAL.

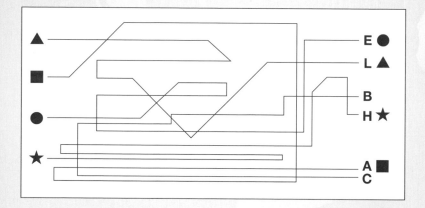

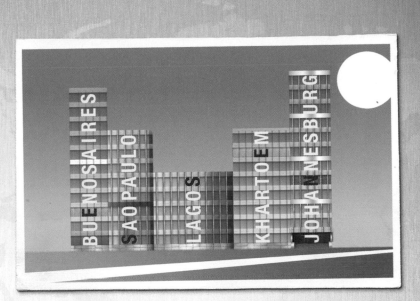

Pages 16 to 19

The building heights in the text correspond to the number of letters in the names of locations on the map on pages 24-27, and the lit-up floors are which letter in the name is intended to correspond to the name of the key location:

(A tower stood at the front, eleven storeys tall, with a walkway between the sixth and seventh floors, and a lit-up third floor) =BU**E**NOS AIRES

(The next building was smaller: eight levels, with a gap after the third, and only the ground floor illuminated) = **S**ÃO PAULO

(The shortest building came next, with the top of its five storeys lit up…) =LAGO**S**

(Next came an eight-storey building, its seventh floor aglow)= KHARTO**E**M

(…and finally, twelve full storeys of homesick scientists, its fifth level illuminated) =JOHA**N**NESBURG

Which spells **ESSEN**.

SOLUTIONS

Page 20

Using the cipher key from the newspaper in the prologue, the numbers translate to **FOUR SIX ZERO TWO**.

20	5	9	1	18	7	17	22	10	1	5	23	13	5
F	O	U	R	S	I	X	Z	E	R	O	T	W	O

Pages 24-27

Used for the building puzzle on p.16-19.

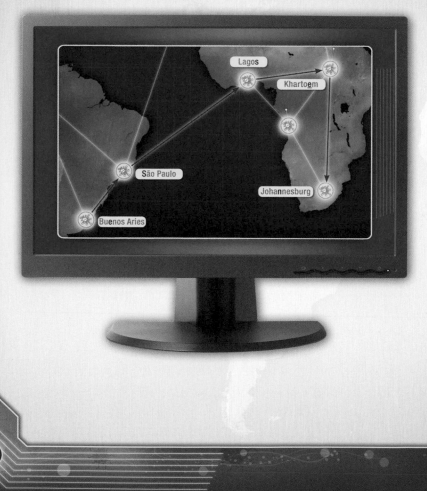

CHAPTER 2

Page 30

The display is reversed, showing the segments that should be missing, and should read...

SAUNDERS.

Pages 32-37

The virus name **D8 C1 T1** shows how many resources are available.

The correct use of the resources is:

Containment specialist = **1 Chartered flight + 1 Drive.**

Medic = **1 Transfer + 2 Drives.**

Generalist = **2 Drives.**

Researcher = **3 Drives**.

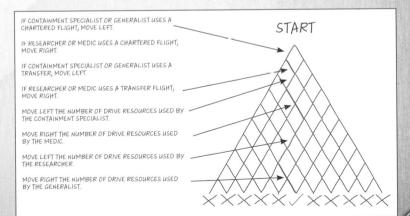

IF CONTAINMENT SPECIALIST OR GENERALIST USES A CHARTERED FLIGHT, MOVE LEFT.

IF RESEARCHER OR MEDIC USES A CHARTERED FLIGHT, MOVE RIGHT.

IF CONTAINMENT SPECIALIST OR GENERALIST USES A TRANSFER, MOVE LEFT.

IF RESEARCHER OR MEDIC USES A TRANSFER FLIGHT, MOVE RIGHT.

MOVE LEFT THE NUMBER OF DRIVE RESOURCES USED BY THE CONTAINMENT SPECIALIST.

MOVE RIGHT THE NUMBER OF DRIVE RESOURCES USED BY THE MEDIC.

MOVE LEFT THE NUMBER OF DRIVE RESOURCES USED BY THE RESEARCHER.

MOVE RIGHT THE NUMBER OF DRIVE RESOURCES USED BY THE GENERALIST.

START

SOLUTIONS

Page 39

Following the path, you collect **LSTHWEI**. These can be rearranged to spell **WHISTLE**.

Page 41

Y = **5**, E = **1**, Q = **8**.
815+885+185=1885.

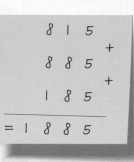

CHAPTER 3

Page 46

The third number is the first minus the second so the answer is **2**.

Pages 48-53

The colour order of the workers left to right is **RED BLUE RED GREEN RED**. This shows the path to take moving along the blueprint's walls, giving you **TS105**. This is the train number for **Sóng Thần**.

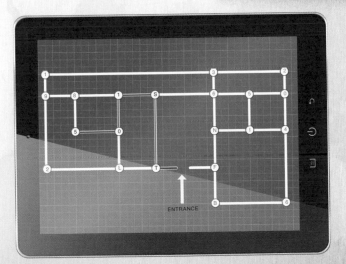

Pages 54-57

See the solution for page 62-63.

Page 59

The codes give you **Cronch**, **Break**, **Plang**, **Tasty** and **Munch**, the underlined letters on their packets spell **HELTH**.

D1 = H
A3 = E
C1 = L
B3 = T
A2 = H

Pages 62-63

Each number explains which type of material to use on the trees on page 54. They connect between the white numbers on the trees, forming the physical shape of a different digit in each case, which is **9315**.

CHAPTER 4

Page 66

Red = **5** Black = **3** Blue = **1**
Yellow = **6**.

🦠	💥	💢	11
☀	🦴	🦠	12
💢	🦴	☀	10
14	5	14	

🦠 =5
💢 =3
🦴 =1
☀ =6

Pages 67-73

See p77-p79.

Page 75

Each four digit number on the cards is double the one before it, so the missing numbers are **9056**.

Page 76

Looking at the worn keys shows the password is her surname, **TOKARCZUK**.

Pages 77-79

The letter on p73 explains there is one successful case, and there is a list of test subjects on p79.

On p69 each petri dish has a different number of empty areas. The name of the successful cocktail comes by taking the first letter of the name of the dish with 1 drip, the second letter of the dish with 2 drips, etc. This gives **DLerE**. Ignore any test subjects without that cocktail.

The poster on p67 says 'don't feel blue' and to eliminate sadness. There is a sad blue worker on p77 and a flask with blue liquid on p70-p71, so this indicates to must ignore any test subjects that are **34** (the age on the blue flask).

The letter indicates the subject was named either Gerry or Lou, so it cannot be H.Otto and the successful subject with the cure for Blue must be **G.Ludwig**.

Age of Sample:
34

Test Subject Results (Batch 30)					
199825	G. Ludwig	38	29th March	Essen	DLerE-15 ...

CHAPTER 5

Page 82

The bottom line is:

Yellow Black Blue Red.

Pages 83-87

The note on p83 saying **Mo-Mi-Ba-Al** represents the first 2 letters of four cities on the map on p84-p85: **Mo**scow, **Mi**lan, **Ba**ghdad and **Al**giers.

Travelling through these cities in that order note that there are **3 Black** cubes, then **2 Blue**, **2 Yellow** and **1 Black**.

Using the graph on p87, move upwards from each of the coloured numbers in order, then look at what letter codes are opposite the level of the line, to get EP-ID-EM-IC, **EPIDEMIC**.

Moscow - 3 Black
Milan - 2 Blue
Baghdad - 2 Yellow
Algiers - 1 Black

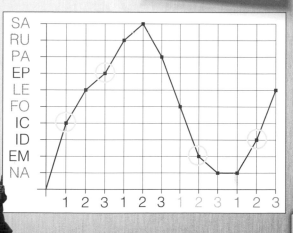

SOLUTIONS

Pages 90-93

See p96-p99.

Page 94

The number of columns in the panels is first half of the number and the total number of segments is the second half, so the final panel generates **03.42v.**

23 MARCH –

26 MARCH – GRIPAY

17 MARCH – togglar

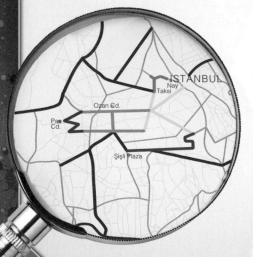

Pages 96-99

On p99, it explains there's a three letter code for the right plan.

On p89 three words are in bold, **roof**, **foul** and **peak**. On p93 these words are used in 3 text messages that were sent on the **23rd, 26th** and **17th**.

On p91, looking at those dates in order on the band poster gives three logos for **Eymen Ersoy, Gripay** and **Togglar**. These have uniquely shaped letters with dots on them.

On p96-p97 there is a map, taking the shapes of the letters from the logo and applying them to the map in order the dots will indicate three letters from words on the map: Pa**s** Cd., Ozan **C**d., and **I**STANBUL, giving you **SCI**, indicating **Plan E.**

CHAPTER 6

Page 102

See p108-p115.

Page 103

Spider plant = **200mls**

Dieffenbachia = **30mls**

Violet **= 20mls**

30x20x30 = **18,000mls**

spider plant = 200mls

dieffenbachia = 30mls

violet = 20mls

My Lima plants

x x = 18,000 mls

Page 104

Each bold number is a multiple of the two either side, so the missing number is **90.**

60
6   10
30   90)
5   9
45

Page 105

The solution is **691**.

Locker Codes Reminders

Reeves 8 + 5 − 3 = 10

Lethem 6 − 9 + 1 = -2

Voss 7 − 0 + 2 = 9

= 9   = 14   = 4

Pages 108-115

On p108 the letter hints one of the subjects on p112-p113 has the cure. The words 'it's a starting place at least!' indicate starting at a city on the map, then travelling to a destination city, which will indicate the subject's location.

Using the International Code of Signals, Margo spells out "**LOS AN**" (*Lima Oscar Sierra Alfa November* – she deliberately misspells "Romeo"), at which point she cuts the letter short, just as she's about to mention the next letter, Golf. The starting place is therefore Los Angeles.

Margo mentioned that she hadn't left the lab in August, but her collection of bus tickets on p112-p113 shows this to be untrue. The journeys were identical but bought on six successive days at different times. By "studying the hour hand of her wall clock on its long, slow transit", each ticket shows the clock bearing to travel using the map, starting from Los Angeles:

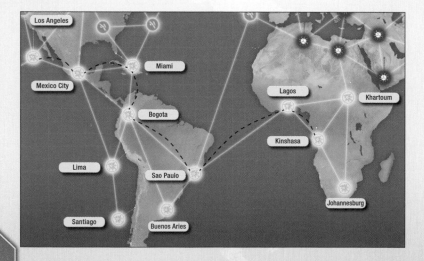

16th August, 3:40 (**Los Angeles** to **Mexico City**)

17th August, 2:45 (**Mexico City** to **Miami**)

18th August, 6:10 (**Miami** to **Bogotá**)

19th August, 4:25 (**Bogotá** to **São Paulo**)

20th August, 1:50 (**São Paulo** to **Lagos**)

21st August, 4:30 (**Lagos** to **Kinshasa**)

The final destination is **Kinshasha**, the location of the successful cure.

There are two patients from Kinshasa listed on the test results. However, one of the tables is a decoy. Margo, knowing that Lethem would be in front of her cat poster (p102), put the correct information on the page that was printed in Cheshire, like the cat from Alice In Wonderland. The 'Never Give Up' poster on p115 is also printed in Cheshire. Therefore, **F. Ngoy** from Kinshasa received the successful cure for Yellow, which was **QzjFl-32**.

Test Subject Results (Batch 150)

209578	F. Ngoy	44	26th October	Kinshasa	QzjFI-32	...

Printed in Cheshire

SOLUTIONS

CHAPTER 7

Pages 119-123

On p119 the cars make the shape of the following numbers: **Yellow = 1, Red = 7, Blue = 0, Green = 4**.

On p123, the solution to the information light colours is **Blue, Yellow, Red**.

Using the colour code from p119, you get the number **017**.

On p121 the road-signs show **Barrackpore** is **17**km away, and is therefore the intended destination.

INFORMATION LIGHTS

बैरकपुर 17 किमी
BARRACKPORE 17KM

Page 124

He is *D) His Son*

Page 129

The only desk that fits all criteria is **#342**.

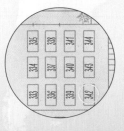

Pages 130-137

As before the aim is to identify the test subject from the list on p137.

On p132 is a tangram. Using the map from p131 it can be identified as **Delhi**, therefore eliminate all subjects not from there.

On p134 the pigpen cypher can be solved by finding the symbols and numbers scattered around the entire chapter and matching their positions on the page (i.e. two numbers in a horizontal rectangle on the lower right corner of a page match with two symbols in a horizontal rectangle on the lower right corner of a page.)

Doing this shows the correct case is **34** years old.

By using the DoBs on p136 it can be calculated that of the two 34-year-olds only **L.Khan** has a birthday that does not fall 30 days before or after any of the employees, and **bBoSD-18** is the correct drug cocktail to cure Black.

Test Subject Results (Batch 186)

| 401175 | L. Khan | 34 | 4th March | Delhi | bBoSD-18 | ... |

SOLUTIONS

CHAPTER 8

Page 141
See p151.

Page 143
His number is **16947439**.

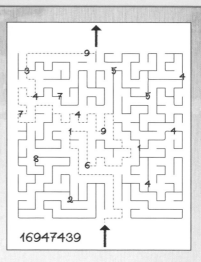

16947439

Page 144
Red- Cog = **1**, Heart = **0** and Star = **8**
Therefore, the answer is **1000**.
Blue - Asterisk = **8**, triangle = **6**
moon= **1**
Therefore, the answer is **1188**.

Pages 146-147
See p151.

Page 149
It's established the two girls did Football and Puzzle Club, and it's stated Hunter did not get in, so **JAMES** is the tap-dancing child.

Page 151

On Page p146-p147 there is a satellite image of many buildings. The 6 lists of directions on the computer screen draw out the shapes of these buildings on a 9x9 grid. U=**Up**, D=**Down**, L=**Left** and R=**Right**.

Each of the six buildings drawn has a number. This gives a list of numbers, which is **26, 17, 18, 14, 24** and **10**.

 Using the code key at the bottom of the computer screen on p151 spells out the name of the bioterrorist, **SOUTAR**. This can be identified as a name of one of the team because of the list of colleagues and their plans on p141.

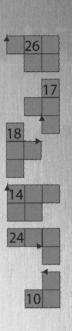

R	R	R	U	U	I	I	U	I	U	=	26	=	S
L	U	R	U	R	D	D	D	L	U	=	17	=	O
D	L	D	L	U	U	U	R	D	R	=	18	=	U
R	R	R	D	L	D	L	L	U	U	=	14	=	T
D	R	U	U	L	L	L	D	R	R	=	24	=	A
D	L	D	R	R	U	U	L			=	10	=	R

S	I	B	L	N	Z	C	Y	G	T	E	J	U	W	R	H	D	K	M	X	O	F	P	A	Q	V
26	16	8	3	20	19	22	6	1	14	13	7	18	11	10	21	5	9	23	15	17	12	2	24	25	4

CHAPTER 9

Page 158

Once you turn the compasses so that N is at the top the blue needle shows the daytime temperature as if was a clock's hand. Flip horizontally and the red tipped needle shows the nighttime temperature in the same way.

Jakarta

The nighttime temperature in Jakarta is **10°**.

Page 161

See p165-p168.

Page 163

Clockwise, the badges are **1976, 6229, 1504** and **4328**.

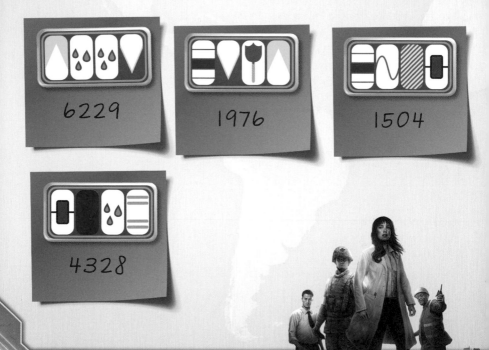

Pages 165-168

On p166-p167 the only key with no lock is key 0, therefore it is the locker key. The text on p168 indicates you must learn a destination. On p161 following the helicopter's paths gives four numbers: **2,4,5** and **9**.

The keys with these numbers on p166-p167 match the following locks: **O, Y, L** and **N**.

However, arranging the helicopter numbers based on the colour order from the left side of Margo's ID card (**Orange, Green, Grey** and **Blue**) gives **5,4,2,9**.

This translates via the locks to **LYON**, the intended destination.

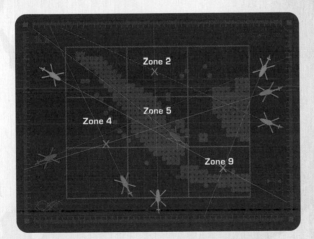

Page 169

The food order is **Apple, Biscuit, Cheese, Peanut Butter, Carrot, Meat**.

CHAPTER 10

Page 174

See p176-p181.

Page 175

The first combination is the locks that are the colour the words are visually, **7732**.

The second combination is the locks that are colour the word itself describes, **4851**.

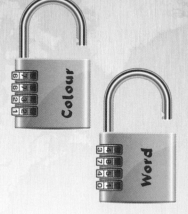

Pages 176-p181

The text on p179 explains that the code for a previous drug cocktail would cure Red.

On p177 the bioterrorist's message gives the clue *EVERYTHIRDLETTER*.

On p174 taking every third letter from the encryption key text at the bottom of the email gives **BLACK1, WHITE2, RED4** and **BLUE8**.

```
Encryption Key
•<<EMBARL4NAFLCRMK2N1UC•
•PSWLKHLZIM5TK0EXE2R3•
•SGRKEEBVDHJ4EA•
•SDB3HL7HUVBE2M8DX>>•

Every third letter
BLACK1WHITE2RED4BLUE8

BLACK 1
WHITE 2
RED 4
BLUE 8
```

On p181, correctly inserting the pill pieces puts the following colours on the following numbers:

1 – **Blue, Red, Red and Black**.

2 – **Blue and Black**.

3 – **White and White**.

4 – **Black and White**.

5 – **Blue and Red**.

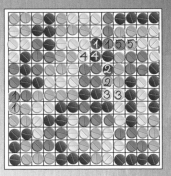

Using the colour values from the encryption key text and add them together gives:

1 – 8+4+4+1= **17**

2 – 8+1= **9**

3 – 2+2= **4**

4 – 1+2= **3**

5 – 8+4= **12**

X	U	Y	C	A
17	9	4	3	12

The message on p177 hints using the newspaper from the bioterrorist, which is on p9 in the Prologue! Using this translates **17,9,4,3,12** into **XUYCA**.

Remembering that Margo thinks Yellow and Red are connected, going back to her previous test subjects on p113 in Chapter 6 shows that **J. Gutierrez's** drug code is **xUyCa-32** and therefore that is the cure for Red.

Test Subject Results (Batch 150)

209578   F. Ngoy   44   26th October   Kinshasa   QzjFI-32   ...

Printed in Cheshire

Pages 182-p185

See p189.

Page 186

The circled words form the numbers 703.

```
B L R V C Q T Y U R P A R V Y N U M U S H V R O N
J R O S E N T H A L F D Y B T H R I V E S A D E C
N A R E K T R A L D G E X A B T U T M P L O W X S
D F H D H U W E Y F S S C R G V X S G C U Y I E Z
X V E C A C U D S L E T H E M D Y R S X V N J G D
O G E C T O C X H F R B I C Z R X R W V J T V T X
X S I C V X C E O X A B C T N E D W Y B M W Z Q P
U D C N Q W N X N K G D K W E H F U E W C B M Z T
O I W J D A A A G A M V S E O T P G M X A F H I R Q
A N P L N U B T G S R D N V H E R O N E C Y B X Q
S G C E F B E T O C B M B E R H E R T F D A Z D S
E C R S B N J R N R E K R A P S N O T P A H S K P
E A D F V G R H J I T H D H V D W F G H C D E U S
S W E C A D S I R E N E E S X C H J Y D W C G Z E
E R V C G S L W D D G H J T D S A D H J K L F C W
O X S X S A V F B H N K F T M D O S A U N D E R S
B W E X E L L D K C W F O C R X S X V D S X V A Z
Z X P C F C F L A P S C D S C E B S E C G J X K E
L J P B V X D D B H G S S S S F H J K K T R V S O D
D E G N B S W W E U B S W G V X L E S S I N G T U
```

Page 188

This is how to assign the resources to wipe out all the cubes from the map on p184-p185.

Edwards - 2 moves: **Kinshasa** and **Johannesburg**.

Bond - 1 move: **Lagos**.

Ahmed - 2 moves: **Mexico City** and **Miami**.

Dale - 2 moves: **Lagos** and **São Paulo**.

Chinyere - 3 moves: **Lima, Bogota** and **Buenos Aires**.

3	Edwards	Start in Khartoum	2 moves
4	Bond	Start in Khartoum	1 move
5	Ahmed	Start in L.A.	2 moves
6	Dale	Start in Khartoum	2 moves
7	Chinyere	Start in Santiago	3 moves

On p182 the position of the monitors indicates which of the lettered cubes on their final destinations should be used to form the name to call, once they have been arranged alphabetically (they are A-E).

Ahmed is on his own and Miami has only one cube, **D**

Bond is on the left of two screens, so it is the left cube, **A**

Chinyere is top right on the group of three, cube **V**

Dale is top left, cube **I**

Edwards is bottom middle, **S**

Therefore, Shepherd must call...**DAVIS**.

PICTURE CREDITS

The publishers would like to thank the following sources for their kind permission to reproduce the pictures in this book.

Original Pandemic Art by Chris Quilliams.
All images © Z-Man Games except the following:

Shutterstock 8, 9, 10 12 13, 14, 15, 16, 17, 18, 20 18, 20, 21, 22, 25, 26, 27, 28, 30, 31, 32, 33, 34, 36, 38, 39, 40, 41, 42, 44, 45, 46, 47, 48, 48, 50, 51, 52, 53, 54, 55, 56, 58, 59, 60, 62, 64, 66, 67, 68, 69, 70, 72, 73, 74, 75, 76, 77, 78, 80, 82, 83, 86, 87, 90, 91, 92, 93, 94, 95, 96, 97, 98, 99, 100, 102, 103, 104, 105, 106, 107, 109, 110, 112, 113, 115, 116, 118, 119, 120, 121, 122, 123, 124, 125, 126, 127, 128, 129, 130, 133, 134, 135, 136, 137, 138, 140, 141, 142, 143, 144, 145, 146, 147, 148, 149, 149, 150, 151, 152, 154, 156, 157, 158, 160, 161, 162, 163, 164, 165, 166, 169, 168, 169, 170, 172, 173, 174, 175, 176, 177, 179, 181, 182, 186, 187, 188, 189

Every effort has been made to acknowledge correctly and contact the source and/or copyright holder for each picture. Any unintentional errors or omissions will be corrected in future editions of this book.